THE WOW FACTOR!

By **T.J. Rohleder**
(a.k.a "The Blue Jeans Millionaire")

Be Sure to Check Out Other Great Titles from the BLUE JEANS MILLIONAIRE LIBRARY:

The Magic Pill
The 2-Step Marketing Secret Than Never Fails!
3 Steps to Instant Profits!
Instant Cash Flow!
Money Machine
The Power of Hype!
Stealth Marketing

TABLE OF CONTENTS

INTRODUCTION:

By T.J. Rohleder

WOW THEM... AND WIN!!!

Congratulations on your decision to read this book. This separates you from all of the other entrepreneurs and small businesspeople who 'claim' they want to make more money, but won't take the time to study a book that can help them do it.

Yes, so many people want the MAJOR BENEFITS of being in business — without going through all of the time, work, and effort to get them. This is true in all aspects of life. People want THE VERY BEST RESULTS, but don't want to pay the price to get them. **And that's sad because business has SO MANY GREAT REWARDS TO OFFER!** It can lead to a life of complete and total freedom and fulfillment. And finding all of the ways and means to make more money can be a great deal of fun!

So what's the secret? That's simple, just become A GREAT MARKETER. This is the key to dramatically increasing your sales and profits. It's the secret that gives you a MAJOR UNFAIR ADVANTAGE over all of your competitors... And once you get good at marketing yourself and your business, you'll discover that...

THIS IS THE GREATEST GAME ON EARTH!

Not only can learning how to become a great marketer make you a lot of money, but it's also VERY REWARDING and a lot of fun!

Marketing is made up of **all the things you do to ATTRACT and RETAIN the largest number of the very best prospective buyers** in your market. That's it. It sounds simple because it is! Of course, like everything else that's most worthwhile, IT'S NOT EASY. This is especially true in today's overcrowded and over-hyped marketplace. But tell me ANY GAME that's easy and I'll show you one boring game that you don't want to play!

Anyway, the fact that learning how to become a great marketer is difficult is THE #1 REASON why none of your competitors will EVER do it. Remember that. Think deeply about that. Then consider this fact: **Your ability to ATTRACT and RETAIN the very best customers in your marketplace is the key to making all the money you've ever dreamed of making.** Sure, there's a learning curve you must go through and it can be a bit painful. But that's THE PRICE you must continually pay to get really good at ANYTHING you want badly enough. And I promise, when you get good at all of the things you have to do to MARKET YOURSELF AND YOUR BUSINESS, you'll have a major, unfair advantage over all of the people and companies who are also trying to do business with the same prospects and customers that you're trying to attract and retain.

So please **let this be your #1 FOCUS** as you go through this book. Have fun reading and thinking about all of the powerful ideas and strategies I'm about to share with you.

Here's What You'll Discover In This Book

This book gives you fifteen of my most powerful marketing secrets that I've used to build my own business. The first chapter is also the title of this book. It tells you how to create 'THE WOW FACTOR!' that can make it easy to get more people to give you MORE MONEY... starting NOW!

Does this excite you? If so — GREAT!!! You should be excited because **getting more people to give you more money is the key to YOUR ULTIMATE SUCCESS!**

IT'S TRUE! The real secret to success in any business is to get MORE PEOPLE to give you MORE MONEY — MORE OFTEN and for MORE PROFIT per transaction. That's it. You could put that on a 5 x 7 card... BURN IT INTO YOUR BRAIN... and then commit yourself to doing whatever it takes to achieve this and become financially set for life!

But I hope you'll do MORE than this. I sincerely hope you'll MAKE THE TIME to go through Chapter One to fully understand some of the most important aspects of this 'WOW FACTOR!' and how it can transform your business and then go through the rest of this book to discover EVEN MORE of the proven tips, tricks, and strategies that can transform your business. Do this and you will have a very real, almost unfair advantage over all of the other people who are trying hard to do business with the same customers you're trying to attract and retain.

And to reward you for purchasing this book, I have...

A great FREE business-building gift for you!

Yes, I have a gift waiting for you that can DRAMATICALLY INCREASE YOUR SALES AND PROFITS! Here's what it's all about: I spent TEN FULL YEARS writing down all of the greatest marketing and success secrets I discovered during that time period. Each day, I took a few notes and, at the end of a decade, I had a GIANT LIST of 6,159 powerful secrets! This list is ALMOST 1,000 PAGES of hardcore money-making ideas and strategies!** **Best of all, this massive collection is now YOURS ABSOLUTELY FREE!** Just go to: www.6159FreeSecrets.com and get it NOW! As you'll see, this complete collection of 6,159 of my greatest marketing and success secrets, far more valuable than those you can buy from others for $495 to $997, is absolutely **FREE.** No cost, no obligation.

Why am I giving away this GIANT COLLECTION of secrets that took ONE DECADE to discover and compile—FOR FREE? That's simple: I believe many of the people who receive these 6,159 secrets in this huge 955 page PDF document will want to obtain some of our other books and audio programs and participate in our special COACHING PROGRAMS. However, you are NOT obligated to buy anything—now or ever.

I know you're serious about making more money or you wouldn't be reading this. So go to: www.6159FreeSecrets.com and get this complete collection of 6,159 of my greatest marketing and success secrets right now! **You'll get this GREAT FREE GIFT in the next few minutes, just for letting me add you to my Client mailing list,** and I'll stay in CLOSE

TOUCH with you... and do all I can to help you make even more money with my proven marketing strategies and methods.

So with all this said, let's begin…

** WARNING: This complete collection of 6,159 marketing and success secrets contains MANY CONTROVERSIAL ideas and methods. Also, it was originally written for MY EYES ONLY and for a few VERY CLOSE FRIENDS. Therefore, the language is X-RATED in some places [I got VERY EXCITED when I wrote many of these ideas and used VERY FOUL LANGUAGE to get my ideas across!] so 'IF' you are EASILY OFFENDED or do NOT want to read anything OFFENSIVE, then please do both of us a favor and DO NOT go to my website and download this FREE gift. THANK YOU for your understanding.

CHAPTER ONE

Let your communications buzz with excitement!

The <u>greatest sin of all</u> is to bore somebody!

Let Your Communications Buzz with Excitement!

When you're a marketer, the greatest sin of all is to bore somebody.

We all know people just put you to sleep, and that's fine on a personal level; it doesn't hurt anything. But you absolutely can't do that from a business and a marketing perspective. **You have to excite people! You have to be enthusiastic! You have to display passion!** So much of the marketing out there now has zero passion. There's no real enthusiasm to it, which perplexes me—because it's a truism that bored people don't buy. Only excited, enthusiastic people buy and keep on buying.

So: how do they get enthusiastic? By *you* getting enthusiastic! **Selling is a transference of emotion, so the more excited and passionate you are about what you're trying to sell, the more excited and passionate your prospects will be.** Remember, people buy for emotional reasons. That's why they do *everything* they do.

So you've got to be excited about every aspect of your marketing. First of all, you've got to find a market that excites you, and then find (or create) something you have true enthusiasm for. Don't just enter a market because of the moneymaking potential. Do it because you love it and can honestly get excited about it. **That love—that passion, that enthusiasm, that energy—will then be easy for you to share**

with other people. The last thing you want to do is try to fake your enthusiasm. Contrary to popular belief, most people can spot phonies instantly. **You need to have a genuine, natural enthusiasm for whatever you're doing, or you'll fail.**

Think about the best salespeople you've ever met. What qualities did they share? I'll bet what you remember most is their passion, enthusiasm, and excitement. Now, those aren't especially rare qualities; most of us can develop them for our true interests. Passion and enthusiasm can be a quiet thing, too. But when you apply it to marketing, however you decide to handle it, you've got to get people excited! **When you write a headline, it has to express your product's biggest, most exciting benefit.** All sales copy and advertising must be exciting and enthusiastic. **If it's flat, you won't make many sales.** There are too many marketing messages out there, so anything that doesn't immediately strike a chord with the prospect is going to get drowned. Whatever you do, let your communications buzz with excitement!

This principle works for just about anything in life. Let's take sports as an example, because it's something that many people are passionate about. Football is probably my favorite sport, and of course I'm a Kansas City Chiefs fan. Let's say it's a Monday morning after an exciting win, and the Chiefs come up in conversation. If I say, "Yep, they played yesterday. It was a good game," well, that's boring, isn't it? And frankly, that's usually the way the Chiefs have played in the past! After a loss, that's the way the conversation goes. But if they win, I'm supposed to be excited. **If I talk in a plain monotone and I'm just factual, I'm not exactly going to infect anyone with my**

enthusiasm and make them want to become a Chiefs fan. "Yeah, they played a game. It was good. They won, and I'm sure glad they outscored their opponent. Did you see that 55-yard field goal? Boy, he barely got that one across the goal line, didn't he? Rah rah rah."

Remember Eeyore, the donkey in Winnie The Pooh? He talks reeeaaalllyyy slowly, and he's always down on everything: "Woe is me." C'mon—no one really wants to be a part of that kind of conversation! So if you're talking sports, you're usually enthusiastic. You're fired up about your team, and even when your team's stinkin' it up, you're fired up about being mad about them stinking! **And so you speak with passion and conviction, with an urgent energy.** You get all jacked up and you're elevated in your conversational tone.

Chris Lakey likes talking politics, and he can get really energetic and passionate about the subject. **Well, when you're selling your product or service, you need to get as fired up as you might by sports or politics.** When you're enthusiastic about something, your heart rate is elevated, and your body language is different; everything goes up a notch. Your communication *buzzes* with excitement.

Chris and I were talking about the health market recently, and discussed how you feel when you experience relief from a long-term health problem. **You tend to be excited about it, and talk to people about it. That's a natural outflow of the experience that you've had at a personal level.** You've found a cure, and want to spread the good news. People who experience something like that tend to be enthusiastic as they share that news.

As a marketer, you have to transfer that face-to-face enthusiasm into other media. Here at M.O.R.E., Inc., we sell by mail, so most of our advertising is done using the printed word. We write a letter and mail that letter to a prospect. **In order to generate interest (and therefore, sales), that letter has to convey the buzz we're feeling about the product or the service we're offering.** If that letter feels like Eeyore talking, if that letter is empty of emotion and void of excitement, the person reading it isn't going to have any fun reading it. They're certainly not going to feel like we're passionate about our own product, and they're probably not going to be interested in buying it.

Let's say I'm trying to sell you a new smartphone. I could say something like, "Hey, the MyPhone 4 makes phone calls. You can check your email on it. You can browse the web. Oh, and it has a built-in camera, so you can take pictures." That might be factual, but it's boring. On the other hand, if I talk about how excited I am about this new device, that enthusiasm may very well rub off on the prospect. Suppose I say, "The MyPhone 4 will do all kinds of things! You can tell it to make appointments for you, and it will! You can tell it you want to text somebody, and it'll just do it! It'll probably even go to the bathroom for you if you really want it to! That's the next app! **I'm so excited about the MyPhone! Everybody should have a MyPhone!** Your boring old flip phone could never do anything like this! This phone will do *everything* for you!" That's how you generate excitement about a product.

In your sales copy, you have to do the same thing. **You want to transfer your buzz to the reader.** If you can get them excited, they're more likely to buy your product because you've conveyed your own enthusiasm, and you've gotten them into a position where they want to feel the results you've promised them. **The only way they can go to the next level is to buy your product or service, so they can feel that buzz directly.**

In my test ads for my book *The Miracle Cure*, which came out in November 2011, I'm using a story of a lady that I've known for about 30 years. Her name is Mary Jones; she's my graphic artist. **Since she restored her body's pH balance, she's experienced some amazing results. In the course of a conversation with her, she said (and these are her words), "I can walk again!"** And I said, "What did you say?" She repeated, "I can walk again!" Then she started telling me about how her legs had been so bad before the treatment that she could hardly walk.

That became the headline for my test ad: "I can walk again!" It's designed to be exciting and catch the reader's attention—which you absolutely have to do, because so much of the marketing out there is just plain boring, and people find it easy to ignore. They have to ignore something, after all, since they're being bombarded with so many messages so constantly.

As I pointed out earlier, **bored people don't buy.** Neither do those who missed your message because they weren't paying attention. **The only people who buy are those you've interested and excited.** So it's up to you to find those biggest benefits in whatever you're selling and convey them to the prospect in the most dramatic way. Give them a story as exciting and hopeful as Mary being able to walk again. They're really going to pay attention to that.

Last but not least, I'll say this: **Start paying close attention to your own emotions.** What excites you when you read other people's ads and sales copy? Use those features as a model. **The marketing materials that get you excited can teach you how to transfer that excitement to your own material, if you take the time to really study them.**

Chapter Two

All marketing lies in two words:

attraction and retention.

Attraction and Retention

All marketing is embodied in just two words: Attraction and Retention. While there are plenty of details to any marketing process, that's all it boils down to: attracting and retaining customers. **Profit is based on drawing in people who keep spending money with you on a regular basis.**

It sounds simple, doesn't it? And it is, really. So many business books overcomplicate the issue; and sure, business *can* get complicated when you have troubles with cashflow and start running out of money. **But anytime you're confused, just go back to this little formula: sell more stuff to more people, more often, for more profit, with greater efficiency**—in such a way that you've always got an eye on the bottom line, without being pennywise and dollar foolish. This is all you really need to know, no matter how much money you want to make. Write it down. Think about it. Memorize it. Do that and the question is not, "Will you get rich?" but "How rich will you get?" Because the money *will* come to you. I committed that formula to memory the first time somebody said it to me, and look at me now!

Remember that customers prefer to go where they're invited—so you have to keep inviting them. You have to break through all of those layers of resistance; they've got a million things going on, they're trying to protect their disposable income, and (at least at first) they couldn't care less about you or your company. **To snag their attention in the first place, you have to stand out above the crowd in an alluring way.** Sadly, many marketers and business owners have never figured that out. Open your eyes! Start looking at all these "me-too" companies, and how they're all doing the very same things. It's almost like they've got a herd mentality, or they're wearing blinders, optimistically assuming that they don't have to attract customers—that customers will just naturally come to them. Remember the movie *Field of Dreams* from back in the 1990s? Many small business people have the attitude expressed in the movie: "If you build it, they will come." They think all you have to do is hang up a sign, and people will flock to you.

For most businesses, nothing could be further from the truth. If you want to attract the best customers, you and your business must be very attractive to those people. People have so many choices these days… and this old idea that the customer is king went out the window a long time ago! Whoever says the customer is king doesn't understand today's market. **Let me set you straight: the customer is *not* king anymore. The customer is a dictator.** Worse, the customer is a child dictator: a spoiled rotten, tired little kid who hasn't eaten or slept enough, who has all the money in the world, and is cranky, demanding, and bitchy. Think about it. Now, I don't mean that in an insulting way; I'm speaking metaphorically. I love my customers. I love to do things to make them happy and give them what they want. **But the bottom line is, the customer has so many options in every field these days that they can afford to be a dictator.**

So if you want to attract the right customers, you've got to work hard to be eye-catching, which means **you've got to offer**

them precisely what they want. And because you need to retain them for as long as possible, you must remain attractive and keep giving them what want the most so they'll keep coming back.

If I ask you what your customers want the most and you can't tell me in a clear, quick way without really thinking about it, then you haven't been thinking enough. And forget all these general answers, like "they want good value." That's a given, and it's too general to really matter. **You've got to know *exactly* what they want. What turns them on?** Why do they buy what you sell, and why do they continue to buy from the biggest competitors in your market—the ones doing the best? You've got to know the answers to those questions! **If you want to succeed in today's market, you've got to do more and think more deeply than most business people do.**

Because you see, most small businesses eventually go under. According to the U.S. Department of Commerce, 95% of all small businesses that start up today will be out of business five years from now. The odds are against your long-term success. And I don't think that's negative at all; you've just got to shoot for that 5% bracket, baby! That's all *I* care about! Even if a company I've put together goes under, I'm just going to start another one. **A true entrepreneur is not offended in any way by these statistics. In fact, according to some other well-known statistics, the average entrepreneur experiences an average of 4.5 business failures before they finally hit it big.** That just goes to show that the only way to really fail is to give up. If you haven't done that, then you're not a failure.

It's all about attracting and retaining customers. That's all marketing is. That's all *business* is. Every business on the planet has two purposes, linked together as one. **The first purpose, of course, is to serve your customers: to give them what they want the most, and to keep giving them more of those things. The second purpose is to make a profit in doing that, so you can keep giving people what they want the most.** To succeed, you've got to stay focused on both every single day. They've always got to be in the back of your mind. If you're not thinking about those things, then you're not thinking.

Now, here's an example I've used a million times, because it's so apropos and everyone understands where I'm coming from when I use it. Think about your favorite restaurant; we all have one. It's easy to see that the secret to success in the restaurant business is to keep customers coming back, to get them eating more meals on a regular basis, telling all their friends and family, bringing in groups they're involved with, and having the restaurant cater their events (if the restaurant has a catering service). **Well, it works that way in any business, really: Internet businesses, mail order, brick-and-mortar stores, etc. In a sense, we're all in the restaurant business.**

Attraction and retention are two sides of the same coin, and they're inextricably linked. **You can't do one and not the other and expect to succeed.** Consider all these flash-in-the-pan businesses that blow up practically overnight; they have no real long-term plan, and so they usually go away as quickly as they come. We've all seen them come and go, like a fad (and often they're based on fads). One of the reasons for that is that they had the ability to attract customers but didn't have the ability to retain them. They might bring in millions of dollars in a short period... but they have no idea what to do with their customers once they have them. Don't get me wrong: there's nothing wrong with raking in the dough with a fad product. **But if you expect to still be a going concern next year, you'll need a follow-up, a back-end product that helps you retain the customers you've already attracted.** Otherwise, your business model is not sustainable.

Most profits come from repeat business. It usually takes more money to acquire a customer the first time than it does to re-sell them a second or third time, because **your marketing costs are heaviest on the initial transaction.** In some cases you're actually buying customers—that is, it costs you more money to acquire a customer than the profit you take in. Sometimes you break even: if, for example, it costs you $1,000 to acquire a customer who then spends $1,000, then you got the customers for zero cost. Anything more that you earn from them is profit. So it's worthwhile to spend good money to bring customers into the fold in the first place.

On the other side of the equation, you sometimes see businesses that have great relationships with their customers—but they just don't have that many of them, because they do very little to attract new ones. As a result, they may have a very small but very loyal customer base of people who know them really well and like them a lot; and while that lets the business do certain things that other companies with more customers can't do, they just don't thrive. Worse, that customer base will inevitably shrink, because customers die, move away, lose their jobs, or just stop buying for one reason or another. **If they don't recruit new buyers, the business will eventually fail.**

Let me repeat: ***both attraction and retention are needed for a successful, thriving, long-term business.*** The 5% of the companies that make it are the ones who figure this out early on. It's not enough just to bring in large groups of new customers, and it's not enough just to have a system for reselling the customers you have. You've got to have both! **Your goal is to keep the bucket full, if you will, so that it's filling at a faster rate than customers are leaking out the bottom.**

All of your advertising should be designed to either bring in new customers or retain the customers you have. If you're not sure how your advertising breaks down, grab a sheet of paper, make columns marked "Attraction" and "Retention," and jot down what you're doing for each. Is this sale designed to bring people in for the first time? Put that on the Attraction side. Does this coupon make a special offer to your existing customers? Put that on the Retention side. Be honest, and see how the list balances out. Do you have too much of one when you need the other? That may be necessary if you need to bolster one of the factors; but **you may find that you're over-emphasizing one at the expense of the other, which may be the root of your problems.** Try to keep both sides balanced, so you're always working to bring in new customers and, at the same time, always working to retain and do more business with your existing customers.

Maybe a spreadsheet or chart will work better for you. The point is, however you do it, just keep track of where all your advertising is going so that you can better understand how well you're retaining and attracting new customers. **If the two factors get too far out of sync, you're mixing up a recipe for failure.**

CHAPTER THREE

Do everything possible to shift the power and get them to chase you — ***rather than you chasing them!***

Let Them Chase You

Do everything possible to shift the balance of power in the business equation so that the customers chase you rather than you chasing them. In order to really understand this principle, you have to realize in your heart that people love to buy things... but they hate to be sold. **So what you have to do is create the illusion, insofar as possible, that they're buying from you without you influencing their decision to so.** Do that, and they'll buy more. This can be a very subtle process, because we're dealing with human emotions here; that's part of what makes marketing more of an art than a science.

So what's the difference between buying and being sold to? The perception of power—of who's in charge of the transaction. **Buying puts someone in a position of power; being sold to takes most of the power away from them.** You can see why most people love one and hate the other. When they buy, it's their choice. The less they feel they have a choice, the unhappier they'll be. Unhappy customers rarely come back to buy more. That said, some may buy anyway for some reason or another; that's why a lot of MLM companies are successful at first. Their only real strategy is for people to exploit their "warm" personal relationships and put people under pressure to get them to join. Some will feel obligated to do so... but they'll never be committed to the business, and as soon as they can, they're going to get out of it. **The only way people are going to be committed**

to anything is if they feel a sense of ownership in it.

So yes, it's a subtle thing; but the more people feel that it's their choice to seek you out, the more they feel empowered and the more likely they are to buy. They love to buy. They love choices. We all do!

Our favorite marketing strategy, which we use whenever possible, is **two-step marketing.** This puts the power firmly in the consumer's hands, because they can get involved or not, as they choose. **Here's how it works:** first, you run some kind of initial lead generation offer where people raise their hands if they're interested. The people who don't never hear from you again; but those who do have qualified themselves for your offer. On the second step, you send the package out to them, and ideally they'll buy. Because here's the thing: people tend to forget that you were the one who approached them first. And you want them to forget that, because it's in your best interest. You want to create the illusion that they're the ones coming after you, rather than vice-versa. **So do all you can to help them feel that *they* sought *you* out.**

In addition, in every type of business negotiation, you have to create the impression that the other party needs you a hell of a lot more than you need them. The power has to be shifted in such a way that they're the one chasing after you because, again, that's what people want. **They like to be the person making the decisions. They like it when choices are theirs.** They like to be the dictator, not the one being dictated to.

There's a famous marketing guy who charges ridiculous rates (thousands of dollars an hour sometimes), and people pay those rates hand-over-fist. But when he first started out, he was flat broke, facing bankruptcy and digging for quarters in the couch. And yet when he had a good prospect who called him up, ready to do business, his first reaction was, "I'm sorry, I'm all booked up this week. Let me look at my calendar next week. Oh, sorry, can't get you in next week either. How about three weeks from next Tuesday?" Now, he said that even when he was practically starving to death! And why? Because desperation is not an attractor factor. Quite the contrary: **people want things they can't easily have. They want scarcity, so this gentleman created an illusion of scarcity... and it worked very well for him.**

The late, great Gary Halbert was famous for telling people that he wasn't accepting any new clients, because he was tired of them. He would say stuff like, "I'm so sick of making millions of dollars for my clients, because they don't appreciate me." Well, it was all just a ruse, a ploy. The more he talked about how sick and tired he was of making his clients a fortune, and how he wasn't accepting anyone new, the more he had people standing in line begging to become his clients... and the more he could charge. **Basically, he ran until they caught him!** Anybody who's ever played the dating game knows that one. Neediness is not an attractor factor. **People always want what they can't have.** The cat always wants to go through the door that's closed.

Some people might cynically point out, "But that's just manipulation. You're manipulating these people!" And they're right. What do you think marketing is in the first place? Just setting up a stand or hanging out a shingle won't necessarily attract people to you. People love to buy stuff, so if you want to sell to them, you've got to create the illusion that they're the ones coming after you, not vice-versa. When they're chasing you, you're in a position of power that you don't have when you're the chaser. **Whoever is being chased has the most control and power in a relationship—any relationship.**

So yes, I say that fully aware of the fact that some people may think that this is manipulative or too over the top—that this isn't a good way to do business. **But I'm talking about mutually beneficial relationships here.** You know, we sell some of our marketing strategies as being "ruthless"; in fact, we have entire books and programs on Ruthless Marketing, and one of things that people always ask us is how that could be a positive thing. Is it good to be aggressive, to think of your marketing as ruthless? And of course, our answer is that **there's nothing wrong with being an aggressive marketer, as long as you're not somehow forcing people to do business with you.** Only the government is allowed to do that.

In a normal business relationship, you provide something of value to someone, and they decide whether or not it's worth their money. If they think so, you make a transaction. **Ruthless marketing just means going after that business as aggressively as you can, knowing that you're working with a prospect who's interested in what you have to sell.** You're not forcing them to buy. It's always their decision to do business with you. Assuming all those things are true, then all that's left to figure out is who controls the chase. The ultimate goal would be to get your customer to chase you.

Earlier, I used the example of Gary Halbert mentioning that he was sick of customers and didn't really want any more. Other marketers have used similar tactics, claiming that they're retiring or cutting down their workload, or they're busy for weeks to come. The reality is, you set your schedule; and if you don't want to do anything between now and three Tuesdays from now, then you can legitimately say you're busy between now and then... even if you're busy doing nothing, which is fine if that's what you want to be doing. You're providing the perception that you're not desperate for business, which is always a good idea. One of the worst things you can do is take a call from someone and say, "Yeah, I'll be there in five minutes!" That removes you from the position of power.

Here's an example. Several months ago, Chris Lakey needed some painting done, so he called a guy who came highly recommended and asked him to come over to make a bid. The guy told Chris that he was out of the state, painting Pizza Huts in Texas, and would be gone for three weeks, assuming the weather held. He said he'd have to get back with Chris when he returned. While that annoyed Chris, he couldn't do anything about it; the painter's schedule was booked until then. **That put him in a position where Chris was chasing him.** He couldn't wait for the painter to get back and bid on the painting job; and that put the painter in a position of power, even though he may never have heard of this principle. He just knew he was busy and couldn't come out to make a bid.

You should always try to put yourself into such a position of power, so that the prospect chases you. You may not be able to get there every time, but it's a laudable goal that you should certainly attempt. As the saying goes, never let 'em see you sweat. **If they sense you're desperate, your price**

drops. If people know you're hurting for business, they have no problem telling you they'll give you less for your goods or services because you've got no demand. On the other hand, if you're extremely busy and don't have time in your schedule for three weeks, your demand goes up, and you can charge a premium because you're in a position where you don't *need* their business.

The key, of course, is to create that perception even when it's not reality. You don't have to lie, but you don't have to tell them why you aren't taking appointments right now. You don't even need to tell them that you're booked and busy if in fact you're not. You can just say, "The first appointment I have right now is in three weeks," or whenever you want your next appointment to be.

The more you can have the customer or prospect chase you, the greater your personal power in the equation; **it makes your customers feel like you're in demand, which makes them appreciate you and what you do for them even more.** It could be as simple as not being instantly available when they call—for example, by not giving them your cell phone number. If you answer the cell every time a prospect calls you, maybe that looks a little like you're desperate. Maybe it looks like you're always available and have the time to talk to them. Maybe instead, you should have people call into a voice mailbox that says, "Call volumes are high right now, and I'll have to call you back," or "I'm sorry, right now I'm away from my desk helping other clients, and I'll need to call you back. Leave me a message." **Anything like that will work—just simple little things that can make customers feel like you're not desperate; like**

you've got plenty of clients, that you don't need them to survive. That puts *you* in the position of power.

That's the position you want to be in! It's not about control in some negative sense, or some form of domination where you overpower them and force them to buy. **You're just putting yourself in a position where you have the power in the relationship; and as a business owner, you want that power.** You don't want the customers to be in control, even though as I mentioned earlier, they're all dictators. They really are! But you don't want *them* to know that. You want to do things to put you in power and give you the control in the business relationship.

Again, marketing is an art, not a science. Some of it can be scientific, **but a lot of it involves dealing with people's emotions, and trying to handle people who don't want to be handled.** People resist any kind of real control, so you need to do everything you can to persuade people to purchase from you. Seizing the initiative in a business relationship is one way to do it.

Chapter Four

Are you a professional or an amateur?

The difference: Amateurs only work hard when they feel like it. Professionals work just as hard whether they feel like it or not.

Be a Professional!

Are you a professional, or are you an amateur? **The difference is this: amateurs only work hard when they feel like it, whereas professionals work hard whether they feel like it or not.** I see so many business "professionals" who are really amateurs, because they work only when they want to. So many of these people are incredibly talented, but they're not serious enough to be professionals... a point I'll return to in a moment. First, let me say this: I'm a copywriter, and I write every day. I only write when I'm 100% motivated and 100% inspired... so I make sure I'm 100% motivated and inspired every morning at five o'clock. Every morning! Seven days a week! Of course, that's supposed to be a joke... but as with any joke, there's some truth to it.

Personally, I have a goal of writing over 100,000 words a month; that works out to about 3,334 words per day. Actually, I try to write close to 4,000 words every day, so that if worse comes to worst and an emergency comes up, I can still make my monthly goal. But I have plenty of days when I do what I call "hitting the wall." It's a term that athletes use when they just run out of energy and have a terrible day.

Some days, if everything works out perfectly for me and I'm on a roll, I can write 4,000 words in less than three hours, start to finish. But then, I also have days when it takes me all day to get those 4,000 words down. I might get up at five in the morning and get started immediately—and not finish until midnight. **I've worked 16 or 17 hours to do the same thing that I can do in three hours when I'm really inspired.** That's the difference between an amateur and professional. If I were an amateur, I might just shrug and give up upon realizing that I'm not going to hit my goal without a lot of hard work; but as a professional, I have to get it done no matter what. I'm trying to be the very best writer I can possibly be, and I've got a huge goal to meet—a goal I take very seriously. Now, there's nobody standing over my shoulder making sure I'm doing my 4,000 words a day. **I keep a daily log,** and I *could* say that I wrote 4,000 words on a particular day even if I only wrote 2,000... but if I did that, I'd be cheating myself.

It all starts with a huge goal, taken very seriously. My writing goal is one example, but for you it may be something different. **Whatever you choose, it must be something big that you work on every day; and it must be measurable, so that you can tell whether you're hitting your milestones or not.** That helps you keep on your toes and push through the bad days that we all encounter, when things go wrong and you just want to give up. Sometimes I have a whole week like that, where I say, "Oh my God! What the hell am I doing?", and I just want to quit. **But I push through, because I believe that you have to be true to yourself, and you do have to set high goals to be a professional.**

There are so many talented people who are much better writers than I am. I can think of one person in particular: a talented copywriter who makes me green with envy. But he probably writes, consistently, 4,000 words a month—maybe 5,000 or a bit more in a good month. Essentially, what I do in a day is about all he writes in 30 days. Although he's an excellent writer, he doesn't work very hard at it—and I believe that in order to achieve your fullest potential, you have to work your ass off. You've got to set really high goals and work very hard, or you'll never achieve your fullest potential.

This guy that I'm talking about has brought in hundreds of thousands of dollars with his sales letters in the past, and yet he's always struggling financially. I've known him now for seven or eight years. He was struggling when I met him, and he's still struggling today; and some months, he barely gets by. There are times when he's almost lost his house; times, in fact, when he's almost lost everything. **I think part of his problem is that he's just not driven enough. He doesn't set high enough goals. He doesn't work hard enough.** He works hard only when he feels like it, when he's moved by the spirit to do so. Well, anybody can do the job when things are easy. **It's when things get really tough, and you rise to the challenge, that you can call yourself a professional and feel that you've earned your stripes.**

That's when you can sincerely pat yourself on the back—and not in some egotistical I'm-better-than-you kind of way. It's not about being better than other people. It's about being the best you can be, and having real reasons to feel good about yourself. In my way of thinking, you have to earn that. **It's a game you play with yourself, and in order to play to win, you have to put in the time.**

I have another friend who's totally driven: I call him a

machine. I know what his goals are because he's told me. I also know that he takes them very seriously. He works very hard from the minute he gets up in the morning to the minute he goes to bed at night. I have every reason to believe that he's going to achieve those high goals he's set for himself. As I was thinking about this topic, I was thinking of these two guys: how both of them are so talented, but only one of them has the true professionalism to push himself on a daily basis. The other does so only when he feels moved by the spirit to do so. He's got the ability; but for some reason, he's just not as driven as my other friend.

There's a lot of value in setting goals and taking those goals so seriously that you work on them even when you don't feel like doing so. **Every time you force yourself to do what you don't want to do, you're achieving something.** To some degree, the achievement is intangible, like all aspects of success; **but it may very well bring you a lot of tangible cash.** This is what separates the true professionals from the amateurs. The real professionals make sure that they push themselves. They're very driven.

There's a book called *Work is My Play* by Wallace E. Johnson, and I recommend that you dig up a copy if you can. Johnson was the co-founder of Holiday Inn, the hotel chain. Now, one of the things he recommends in this book is working half a day... he spends an entire chapter on that. **He says that's the secret to success: just working half a day.** It doesn't matter which half you work, just work half a day. Of course, he's talking about *really* working half a day—a full 12 hours. He's not talking about a 40-hour work week. I've read another quote that says that the difference between a true professional and anybody else is that the professional works that extra 20-30 hours a week.

I know that's a sore subject for some, and it's not an absolute; but giving it your all certainly is. **Pushing through the hard times and continuing to move forward when you feel like giving up... that's what it's all about to me.** Find good positive role models, and follow their lead. If you can't (which may be difficult, because they really are few and far between), then find a whole bunch of negative role models and strive to do the opposite of what they do. You'll have the same result. Keep experimenting. Keep mixing it up. Keep trying a bunch of different things. Just set these goals, like with me and my writing. I have to do 25,000 words a week, at a minimum, to meet that goal. I know exactly what my word counts are every day. I keep track of it all. But I've also mixed it up. I've tried so many different things, and if one thing doesn't work, I go to another one. **I just find ways to keep it fresh and to keep from getting burned out.**

And by the way, it's one thing to work through bad times; it's another to get to a place where you're just totally burned out. That only happens when you don't mix it up, when you don't have some variety in your life. **It happens when you don't try fresh and innovative approaches.** The real strength here is learning how to do something 10 or 20 different ways; even having just five different ways can help.

I think there are some important lessons to be learned in looking at the differences between professionals and amateurs in many different industries. Remember, the basic strategy here is that amateurs work hard only when they feel like it;

professionals work just as hard whether they feel like it or not. An amateur at anything will get flashes of brilliance or excitement that energizes them when they're working on something interesting to them, something that catches their imagination. That's when you'll find them working hard and trying to excel. **Then, what usually happens is that the excitement wanes, and they revert back to the way they were before.** They become a little more apathetic, a little lazier, a little less interested, a little less engaged. They're not as likely to spend the same amount of time on a project that doesn't excite them anymore.

A professional, on the other hand, will work hard because they're a professional, trying to consistently excel at something. Consider a professional athlete—an NFL player, for example. If I played professional football, I would live for game-time. I would strive to be the best that I could be for those three or so hours of play. I would give it all I had, and leave it all on the field. I would try my hardest to win that game, because that's what I really like doing. So, what's the difference between the guy who becomes a 15-year veteran and a rookie who's on the team this year, but out the next year? The veteran is a professional athlete, completely dedicated and sold out to his profession. He spends time and energy in the weight room when all his other buddies are playing Xbox. Instead of watching films of the games, they're at a sports bar drinking beers. The professional athlete knows that the moments where he excels on the field are only possible because of the time he spends in the training room, or in the film room breaking down the strategies of his opponents. It may not be as fun as drinking beer, but of course he's a professional athlete. He wants to play the game.

The Hall-of-Famers, the *professional* athletes, are just as dedicated to the stuff that you and I might find boring as they are to hitting the field on game day. They spend most of their time toning their physical and mental prowess—much more time than they spend actually playing against other teams. The same is true with a professional athlete in any other sport. If they don't practice, if they don't train, if they don't watch the things they put into their body, they're never going to work at their peak. **The athlete who doesn't pay attention to their training program is always going to be an amateur athlete rather than a professional, even if they do get paid**—and if that's the case, they won't get paid for long.

It's important to understand the difference between amateurs and professionals. Now, there are a lot of different opinions on what things comprise this difference. Most people just see the legal or technical classification between an amateur or a professional: **pros are paid, amateurs aren't.** In college sports, for example, the players are amateur athletes in the sense that they aren't getting paid. But I think that's the wrong way to look at it. A lot of college athletes are just as dedicated as the professional ones, and a sense, they *are* getting paid, often with scholarships.

It's not necessarily about the time you've spent in the game, either. To equate that to marketing, you could be a 20-year amateur in your field. Perhaps you've been in the business for a long time, but you've never taken that step forward into the professional realm; instead, you've been dabbling all this time, never taking it seriously. Maybe you've always kept your full-time job, while you've played around in marketing—because you've never been committed to it long-term. **By most accounts, by the time you spend 20 years doing something, you ought to be a professional. But that's not always true.**

On the flip side, maybe you've only been in your business for six months or a year, but you're going at it full-bore. **You've already jumped beyond amateur status, because you've dedicated yourself to being the very best you can be at your business.** You're part of the 5 AM Club: you're one of those people up early every morning, drinking pots of coffee to get all jacked up in caffeine so you can pump out the most possible production in your day. You're like that athlete who spends 10 hours a day in the gym: you're doing what it takes, and working just as hard as you can for the moments when you're in the game. **It's not about time served; it's about dedication.**

Part of the difference between a professional and an amateur is mindset. Are you dedicated to business? Are you dabbling at it, or are you committed to success? Have you decided that you're going to make that shift from a part-timer to a full-timer, from a tire-kicker to a pro? Are you going to do whatever it takes to succeed, or are you going to keep that fallback? Are you going to have an insurance policy? You know: "If this doesn't work out for me, I'll just do that instead. I've always got that," or "I'm going to keep my full-time job because I'm afraid to go all out in business."

Simply put, the difference between amateur and professional is how hard you work, even when you don't like to work—when you're doing things that you don't necessarily like to do, or you don't get the most enjoyment

out of. Again, consider the football analogy. If you play football, are you willing to work as hard in the gym as you do on the field on Sunday? Are you willing to work just as hard doing all the little things that make a big difference in your business as you are on the things that seem to be the most important? It's how you handle yourself all those other times that determines whether you're going to remain an amateur or become a professional. It starts in the mind, but then moves quickly into the actions you take to accomplish your goals. Having those goals is one thing; setting out to achieve them is another entirely. So, amateur or professional? Only you know the difference in your own business, in your own attitudes, and in the results you're achieving.

And remember this: every day is a do-over. You're going to have days when you miss the mark, and that's okay. Don't beat yourself up, because that doesn't help. Just recommit. This is just an ideal you shoot for; you won't always score a bull's-eye. There's a wonderful book by George Leonard titled *Mastery*, and a lot of what I'm discussing here relates directly to what you'll read about in that book. Leonard talks about dabblers, people who just play around in things. They're not really committed, so the first time something gets a little difficult, they do one of two things: they start coasting, or they just give up and go on to something else. There are plenty of people that do that in business; after all, 95% of all small businesses fail within the first five years. **A failure to achieve a professional mindset is a large part of the reason why they fail.**

Chapter Five

"Marketing is simply a combination of math and psychology."

— Dan Kennedy

Marketing = Math + Psychology

As the great marketer Dan Kennedy once pointed out, "Marketing is simply a combination of math and psychology." There's a little more to it than that, but Dan's quote goes directly to the heart of the matter. So let's break that out a bit.

First of all, as I've discussed in other Ways, marketing is all the things you do to attract and retain the largest number of the very best prospects in your market. I think that's a definition that every marketing expert would agree on, although they'd all want to add their own two cents to it. **Within that premise, all you have to do is attract enough of the right people and get them to rebuy a large enough amount of whatever it is that you sell for the most profit per transaction, for the longest period of time.** That's marketing and marketing strategy in a nutshell—it's all as simple as math and psychology. And the math is simple math: how much something costs versus how much you make.

One of our secrets here at M.O.R.E., Inc. is that **we use two-step marketing as our primary marketing vehicle.** In STEP NUMBER ONE, we try to attract the best-qualified prospective buyers for whatever it is we're selling. In STEP NUMBER TWO, we spend as much money as we profitably can to make that sale, knowing that if we did our job right in the first step, we have a good chance of making back all that money and more. As long as you're working with highly qualified prospects, and you understand enough of the psychology behind their drive to buy and the strategies necessary to convert leads to sales and sales to repeat buyers who become customers for life, then you almost can't spend enough money on Step Number Two.

Understanding and applying that mix of math and psychology gives you a competitive advantage, because most marketers just don't get it. Remember that P.T. Barnum quote: "Most people are trying to catch a whale by using a minnow as bait." Metaphorically speaking, that means that everybody's trying to make the most money they can... but they're trying to do it for the least amount of money possible. They're trying to apply low- and no-cost strategies that don't make a full impact on the people they're trying to sell to. But in order to make a big ticket sale, you have to kill a bunch of trees—that is, **you've got to write long-form sales letters as part of a marketing sequence that continues to go after the prospects and stays after them relentlessly. All of that costs money.** That's the math part. Psychology involves getting inside the heads and hearts of the people you want to sell to. **You need to know why they buy, and what it is they're really looking for.**

Here at M.O.R.E., Inc., we sell business opportunities. Somebody who doesn't understand the particular market segment we serve might think that people are just looking for business opportunities because they want to make more money; but it goes way beyond that. There are many factors in play, both subtle and obvious, and that's true for any marketplace. You have to figure out what those are for your market: **what do the customers really, really want? Realize that people buy mostly for unconscious reasons...** and they may be quite unaware of the causes of their own behavior. **So *you* have to figure out these things, since you damn sure can't ask them.** They don't know. In the course of talking with enough of your customers, and listening and reading between lines, and looking for the commonalities in their behavior and the things they say, you'll ultimately get a handle on it.

Now, you have to think about all the positive reasons why people buy what you sell, but you have to think of all the negative reasons, too. Look at the three F's: **What are their biggest fears, failures, and frustrations?** Often, those are the things that really drive the sale; **the plain fact is that people are often more motivated for negative reasons than positive reasons.** So try to get behind their eyeballs and become the customer.

It's said that if you want to catch a fish, you have to think like a fish. I'm not sure anybody can really think like a fish, but I understand the concept here. There's an old quote that goes, "If you want to sell what Johnny buys, you have to see things through Johnny's eyes." As dumb as it sounds, I like it because it's easy to remember, and it raises a cogent point. **You have to *become* the customer to understand all the emotional reasons why they buy what they buy.**

Let me tell you a few stories about how we use math and psychology in our business. I've already explained that almost all our marketing is two-step marketing, where the first step is to get highly qualified prospects to take an initial small step—to raise their hand, so to speak. That step could involve buying something for a low price; or, they might have to jump through some other hoops in order to qualify for the second step, so we're more likely to sell our offer to them. You have to set the bar fairly high just to keep out the curious and the tire-kickers, because you want only those prospects who are genuinely interested in your product and may actually buy.

We use direct mail for the most part, which is very expensive. A lot of marketers are turned off by direct mail because they only look at the cost. They don't look at other very important elements, such as how much money you can make from it. **We love direct mail because it gives us total control of the process...** or about as close to total control as you can get. It's a disruptive kind of marketing, unlike an email you can ignore. **You can't necessarily ignore direct mail.** Although most people separate their direct mail over the trashcan, they still have to look at it before they throw it away—and there are all kinds of things you can do to encourage people to open your envelope, once they have it in hand.

And again, while direct mail is very expensive, remember the math part of the equation here. **It doesn't matter how much something costs up front; it only matters how much money it makes you.** If you make $1,000 on a $100 mailing, that's a heck of a return. We do a lot of complicated, expensive follow-up sequences, because they're profitable. **We go after those leads aggressively.** We like to joke that we go after them until they buy or die. The point is, we spend a lot of money on our offers, and that doesn't really matter to us, as such. *What matters is how much money we make.* **We're willing to spend more money than most companies, because it gives us a competitive advantage.**

As far as the psychology aspect goes, we're always trying to get behind our customers' eyeballs and figure them

out. And we always have to keep in mind the fact that the market does change. When we go back and look at stuff that we did 10 or 15 years ago, it becomes obvious that there's no way we can rerun some of that today without making some dramatic changes. In fact, Chris Lakey recently took a sales letter that we did 15 years ago, from one of our most successful promotions ever, and had to completely redo the whole promotion—because the market has changed so much. Whether it's evolved or devolved depends on who you ask at any given moment, but either way, it's not the same market it once was. **So you have to make a serious effort to know the customers—and never, ever assume that they remain static.**

This tactic of really knowing the customer is, I think, the one thing that's made us the most money in this business—I'd even go out on a limb and say it's made us more money than everything else combined. In fact, it was our entry into the marketplace. For years, you see, I was a customer in this marketplace. I was buying from all the people we later went into the business to compete against. Like the old childhood taunt goes, "It takes one to know one." We had a good grasp on the marketplace psychology because I was a member of it already.

That's why whenever you start a business, you need to choose a market you already understand very well. Then strive to know your customers even better than they know themselves. Anytime you get confused, just return to this first principal. And let me point this out: the more determined you are to master something, the better you want to get at it, the more confusion and frustration you're going to face on the road. **So every time you feel bewildered, take a deep breath, pull back,**

and look at the basics. Remember: it's as simple as math and psychology. That aspect of the marketplace never really changes.

Let's take a closer look at the sales letter that Chris Lakey is so brilliantly reworking. He's changing the format: he's taking it from a successful but outdated print format to a modern movie format, delivering the same content in a form that people can watch online on their computers. It's an interesting process, and recently, as part of his research, he was watching a video clip about someone else who did what he's doing, using some of the very same strategies. **The company that did so reported that just that one move, from print to video, increased their sales revenue from that offer by $80 million in one year.** Obviously, this is a huge company to begin with, or they wouldn't be doing that kind of volume. Who it is and what their offer was isn't important; **the point is that they were able to profit incredibly from a simple change in the way that they presented their information.** And according to the presenters of this case study, one of the reasons this happened was because of this combination of math and psychology.

One of the reasons we switched to a movie format was because it was a cheaper way to deliver the message. **We can have people watching the movie all day online, and the cost is very minimal, as opposed to printing up and mailing thousands of copies of a long-form sales letter.** There's a lot of psychology behind the switch as well. People are used to getting news in video format. Think about how long we've been watching news on TV. Even online, people tend to look at video-formatted media as news, whereas if someone gets a sales letter in the mail, it's more easily perceived as a sales pitch. **When**

people watch a video, even if it's a total sales pitch, it feels like it's information. It's similar to what happens in a live seminar setting, where someone is platform selling. There's just something different about seeing a person on video or on stage. **It has a different credibility factor than if you're reading something they mailed to you.**

Making money in your business boils down to your ability to profitably sell your product or service to your marketplace. How do you do that? Well, there are all kinds of methodologies and systems that you can learn and use; but in the end it all comes down to whether you did a good job of convincing your prospects that they should do business with you. The numbers determine whether you have a viable business model or not: there's a cost to doing business, and a cost in bringing in new customers, and a cost to re-selling to existing customers. **Can you successfully sell to enough prospects and do enough to secure existing customers to make a profit?** That depends largely on your model, which influences the numbers involved. In some instances, you need high volume because you have a low ticket cost. If you're only selling something for $25, you need a whole lot of sales to make a million dollars, whereas you'll need a lot fewer if the item is selling for $1,000.

So what are your goals? How much income are you trying to make? If your business is earning you a million dollars a year, how much of that are you keeping? That depends on all kinds of things: overhead, fixed costs, variable costs, and the number of promotions you have. **The numbers will determine whether it's viable for you to continue doing things the way you're doing. These kinds of things go into the math of your**

business. That's all fairly easy and straightforward to figure out.

Psychology is a different animal. **Regardless of industry, regardless of what you're trying to sell, knowing your customers is one of the most important parts of your marketing strategy.** If you don't know who your customers are, if you haven't gotten inside their heads enough to know what they like, then how can you serve them well enough to make a profit? **You need to know what they respond to, what their fears are, what their challenges are, what they want out of life, what they need out of the relationship you're trying to build with them.** If you don't do all those things and know all those things, you're at a disadvantage when trying to sell to them.

Consider the business of selling cars. Let's say you have your average four-door sedan, maybe a bit souped-up. If your prospect is a college-aged kid and he's looking for a sports car, then you know in that moment that he's more interested in horsepower than safety. Therefore, that's the benefit you tout. On the flip side, a mom who comes in with her two kids, looking for a family car, is going to be less interested in the muscle behind the car and more interested in the safety features; so with her, those are the features you emphasize. **You pitch the exact same car differently to the two different customers, emphasizing different benefits, because you understand the psychology behind their needs.** That's applied marketing psychology.

Now, the car market is a unique marketplace, because you're selling the same products to all different kinds of people. Most marketplaces don't work that way, because the customers and prospects are all very similar; there are some differences, of course, but mostly they're buying your product or services for just a few reasons. **Still, you need to get inside their minds, so you know what those reasons are—to the point where you can recite those reasons back to them without thinking twice.** That's how you get them interested in your offer. If you approach a prospect with the wrong message, because you haven't mastered the psychology of selling to that particular marketplace, you're not likely to make a sale. Even if you get the message right and hit them at the wrong time, you're probably going to strike out. Similarly, even offering a message that's just a bit different from their needs and expectations can hurt you.

Let's say you have an investment company, and you're selling information on investing to people who are mostly looking for security in retirement. Maybe they're a little older, and they're not looking to build their nest egg as much as protect it. If you go to those people with an aggressive growth fund that offers both high risk and high reward, they're probably not going to be as interested; they're looking for safer, more secure money management strategies. **Remember: the way you sell the most to people is to know what they're looking for.** You need to be able to speak to them on their level, based on their goals and desires, so it's absolutely imperative that you do your research and get to know those people on a deep level.

Sometimes, those of us in the marketing business (and industry in general) have a bad reputation, because people think we're somehow forcing our wills on an unsuspecting populace—that somehow, because we're marketers, people who transact with us must have been coerced or forced into buying what we sell. That's true no matter what you're selling. If you're an aggressive restaurateur, and you do better than everybody else in getting people into your restaurant, some people will think you're somehow coercing people to eat there. If you have a dry cleaning or carpet cleaning business, and people are choosing to do business with you because you're an aggressive marketer, then somehow you must be getting people to do business with you that otherwise wouldn't have. And that may be true—**but you didn't accomplish it through any form of coercion.**

The reality is that in a free society, people do business with whoever they want to. It may be that an aggressive marketer is doing a better job at hustling the business and getting people to choose to do business with him, but people are still choosing. **The way you get people to choose you over your competitors is by combining math with psychology—by knowing what people want the most, and giving it to them in a way that makes you a profit.** They're still making the decision to buy from you, but you're giving them incentives to do so based on what you know about them and their behavior.

There's nothing coercive about good marketing. People buy what they want to buy. You're just making it available to them, and if you're a better marketer than your competitors, you'll get more business. **You use math and psychology to your advantage, then adjust and tweak it to get the math to work in your favor.** That's what it's all about.

Chapter Six

Our job as marketers is to *attract* the right people and *repel* the wrong ones.

Attract and Repel

Our job as marketers is to attract the right people—and repel the wrong ones. In the previous Way, I talked about using psychology to attract customers, and I'm going to get back to them shortly. But first, let's focus on repelling the wrong prospects.

Five or six months ago, we did a promotion where we sent a little postcard out to our customers. It was totally blind, but the response on this postcard was phenomenal. We were excited by the response... but then our back-end conversion sucked. In other words, we generated a whole bunch of interest in our offer, causing plenty of people to raise their hands and say, "Yes! Send me your package." **But very few people bought in the second step of our promotion, because we didn't do a good enough job of repelling the poor prospects.**

Success in marketing is all about attracting the *right* people, the ones who are really qualified for the offer and are most likely to buy. Often, then, you have to purposely erect some barriers so you can get rid of the people you don't want. One of the ways we've done it in the past with expensive offers was to tell people, on the first step of our two-step marketing process, that the cost was approximately equal to that of a trip to Vegas, or a good used car, or maybe a really nice home entertainment center—something like that. These were cases where we didn't want to flat out tell them the price, but we did want them to see right away that it would cost them a few thousand dollars to get started. **In a case like this, the ones who simply don't have a few thousand dollars to spend, or who don't want to spend that much, disqualify themselves.** We know they're disappointed, but hopefully we've burned them off and sent them on their way. We only want to attract people who are open to the idea of spending a few thousand dollars.

This concept of requiring people to leap through hoops to qualify themselves for our high-end products and services has worked very well for us. Years ago, we had a promotion that did so well on the front end that we actually filled up an Excel spreadsheet. I didn't even know you *could* fill one up; but we had something like 77,000 leads on this promotion. We were working with these experts in Canada; one day, Chris and I were on a conference call with them, and we told them that we were basically sending out postcards and asking people to call a number and listen to a 15-minute recorded message. These guys told us, "Hey, we love your postcard, but get rid of that 15-minute message. Nobody is going to listen to a 15-minute message." Well, Chris and I laughed to ourselves, and we didn't try to argue with them because we were trying to be respectful. The truth was, we were simply generating too many unqualified leads with the postcards and the 15 minute message. The real joke is that the next time we did it, instead of a 15-minute message, we were going to go to a 30-minute message. **If someone isn't going to listen to a 30-minute message, they're not going to buy anyway.** It's a good idea if you do things like that to throw obstacles in people's way.

Recently, we had a promotion that worked really well for us; in fact, I don't know why we haven't redone it yet! We made people go and listen to an online presentation that was more than an hour long. **At the end of that presentation, we gave them a phone number to call—so the only people who got that special number were those who listened to the entire recording.** And then they had to call a *second* phone number. And sure enough, it worked very well. Money's still coming in every month on that promotion.

Years ago, when we had our *Dialing for Dollars* program—this was back in the early 1990s—we had one distributor who was making almost three times more money than we were. And we were doing *very* well. Our company was just getting started; we were a couple of years old at that time, and we were bringing in a couple of million a year. Well, this one distributor was running ads all across the country, and we knew he was making $5-6 million a year because of all of his wholesale orders. Well, you know what? **He was violating everything we told him to do.** We were like those guys from Canada, thinking we knew it all. We were telling him that his recorded messages had to be about three minutes, and his were twice that long—or more. And they were just so boring, so monotone. I asked him about that. Now, you can't argue with success; so I didn't try to do what those guys from Canada did with Chris and me. I just asked, "Jay, why are your messages this way?" He basically said, "Look, if somebody won't listen to my long and boring messages, then they're not a good prospect." **There were some other specifics to it, of course, but basically he was putting barriers up, trying to repel the wrong people so he could attract the right ones.**

You can also use money as qualifiers; that is, you can make people spend a little more to prove that they're the right people for your offer. **If they're not willing to spend a certain amount of money, then they're probably not a good prospect; simple as that.** Sometimes you play up the negative aspects of whatever it is you're selling, trying to burn them off a little bit. If they can't handle those few negative things, chances are they're not going to end up being the kind of customer you want anyway. In other cases, you use long-form sales copy. That little, tiny postcard that got such phenomenal response for us—well, if I'd written a longer letter, I could have done a better job of selling. I could have told people more to help them qualify themselves. It would have been less blind. I would have received fewer leads, but the conversion rate would have been higher. Remember, it's all about how much money you spend versus how much money you make. **Often, you want fewer leads so that you can spend more money on those leads once you get them. You can then convert more of them and make bigger overall profits.**

Again, attracting the right customers, and knowing what messages will get their attention and what they'll bite on, is what's truly important—more so than trying to save money on the initial sale. Yes, you want to reach them as economically as you can, by offering something they can buy for low cost so that they're spending a little money in the beginning. This is very important with new customers. On the other hand, as a rule of thumb, we'll offer free reports, free DVDs, free audio CDs, and the like if we're reselling something to our existing customers. To them, it's "Free, free, free!" **But when dealing with people who have never done business with**

us, we always make them pay at least a little money. Sometimes it's just a dollar. A dollar doesn't seem like much, but again, it's something. Some people are unwilling to part with a buck; and if that's true, what makes you think they're ever going to end up being good customers? They're not.

There are some marketers who pride themselves on having these huge lists—but their lists are lousy. They've got no relationships with the people on those lists. Their lists are a bunch of deadbeats, people who don't buy. **It's not the size of your list that matters, but how qualified the people on that list are, and your relationship with them, and what you did to make sure you attracted the right ones and repelled the wrong ones.**

There's a line in the movie *Jerry Maguire* that I think is appropriate here. Most people remember the movie's "Show me the money" scene; that's the one that sticks out, and it's the one you hear that quoted most often. But there's another line in that movie during the scene where Jerry is getting fired. Jerry writes this mission statement, as he calls it; of course he's jeered for it, and then his boss invites him to dinner and fires him for writing it. One of the things the boss says is, "You put it on paper: fewer clients, more relationships." Jerry's idea is that the business has become something it wasn't supposed to be in the beginning. **It needs to be more about relationships; it needs to be about doing business the right way. It's not just about the numbers.** And that got him fired.

A lot of businesses tend to focus on attracting as many people they can, whether consciously or subconsciously. They begin to feel that they have to bring in as many people as possible to succeed; and the thought of doing anything that would throttle that is outside their imaginations and outside their thinking. They can't picture any scenario by which they would intentionally try to repel business. But you have to. Jerry Maguire's concept of **"Fewer clients, more relationships" is the kind of strategy you need to make the most money.** You can make much higher profits with smaller numbers of well-qualified people than you can with huge numbers of poorly qualified ones. How can you profit when you're overwhelmed by thousands or millions of tire-kickers who aren't interested in spending money—who only responded because you made it easy to? A million "un-leads" aren't going to do you any good. They're just going to cost you money, time, and energy.

You need to repel everybody except for the comparatively small group of people most likely to do business with you. **You need to get out of the mindset of thinking that you need big numbers to make big money.** What you really need is a group of the very best prospects. Our job as marketers is to figure out the right ways to attract the largest number of those people possible. Now, it would be wonderful if you could have a million great customers. But because that's not reality, what you really want is as many as you can get... and the same strategies that draw them in should repel everybody else.

At the very least, you need to require them to jump through a monetary hoop. You must say, "I'm happy to share this with you, but it's going to cost you. I want to ship it to you at your cost, not mine. So if you'll just pay $10 to help with printing and shipping, I'll send it to you." Or even, "I just need a dollar to prove you're serious." In some cases we've sold what was essentially a sales letter for as much as $20. **Of course, we always do it with a money-back guarantee,** so that if you get our report and don't like what you see, you can just let us know and we'll send you your $20 back, no obligations.

We just need to prove you're serious. We don't set up these hoops out of laziness, or because we don't want to put our shipping manager through the hassle of shipping more reports out, or because our printers are too busy and we don't want them to have to print another 1,000 copies of our special report; that's not what it's about at all. **It's about being as productive as we can with the prospects we're attempting to sell to. We only sell to people who seriously want to do business with us.** We can't make people buy from us, but we can get them to request information from us so that they're more likely to buy. We would much rather work with a smaller group of interested prospects than a larger group of tire-kickers or "lookie-loos"—people who may be mildly interested, but aren't committed enough to spend a little money.

If you're selling a $1,000 product and someone won't spend $5 to get information about it, you don't want them. They're probably not going to be a good customer anyway. So, again, don't be afraid to attract the right people and repel the wrong ones. It's actually more important to repel the wrong ones than to attract the right ones; though the truth is, in repelling the wrong ones, you'll often be attracting the right ones as a side effect. If you've got a fishnet and you're trying to catch fish, and you have big holes in your net, you're going to let all the little, tiny fish go. **You're only going to catch the big ones.** You don't want those little fish anyway; you just want them to slide right on through. But the big fish, the ones that make a big tasty meal, the ones you could sell at market—those you want to get stuck in the net. **So you make your net with the right sized holes to let the wrong fish through and let the right fish stick.**

In the marketing world, this means that you design your offers so they repel the bad leads—the people who aren't going to buy anyway. You let them pass right through your net; you don't want them to reply. You only want to net the right kinds of prospects. **The more you can do to separate those two groups, the better.**

Chapter Seven

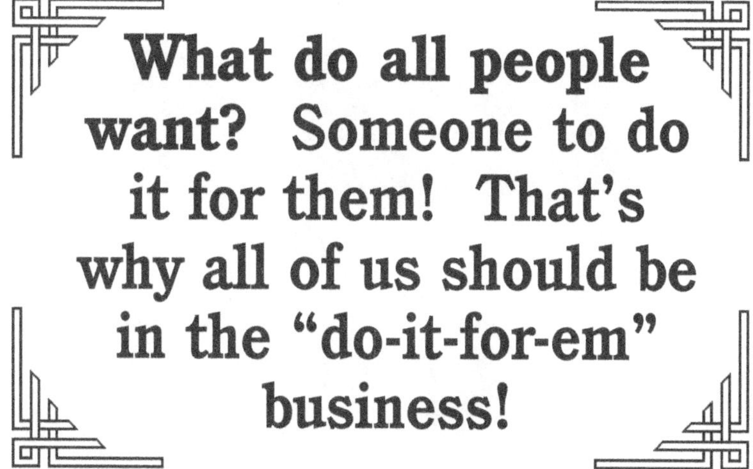

Be in the "Do-It-For-'Em" Business

What do people *really* want? Basically, they want other people to do everything for them. That's why all of us should be in the "do-it-for-'em" business. Here at M.O.R.E., Inc., we started our very first "we do it all for you" service in 2004, and we've kept creating them since. This secret has made us millions of dollars, and it's going to make us millions more. It can do the same for you.

Now, don't assume that people want to avoid all the hard work just because they're lazier than they used to be. Some observers might make that argument, but I believe that it has a lot more to do with the fact that people are just so overwhelmed these days. They're confused and frustrated and exhausted. **They don't want to learn anything new, because they're already subjected to too much information; so what they're looking for is an expert.** In our field, they're looking for someone who can safely guide them in their business decisions.

You have to teach them you're the one that they're looking for, by proving your credibility as an expert in the field. There are specific marketing processes you can use whereby you take a prospect by the hand, so to speak, and lead them through a process of discovery. **You can't just promise to do everything for somebody without telling them your story and sharing your success strategies, your proven track record, and**

making the case for why they should put their trust in you. It doesn't happen by accident. But once you've established that credibility—once you've proven you have the goods and can back up all your promises and claims, that you're not just going take their money and run—well, then, they want you to do everything for them. **And they'll basically throw money at you to get you to do it.**

This a growing trend with no end in sight, and it transcends all marketplaces. It's one of the reasons why outsourcing has become such a huge industry over the last couple of decades. There are so many companies out there that will do a wide variety of things for you, which helps the average entrepreneur enormously. This outsourcing trend gives you the opportunity to hire other companies to take care of most of your needs, so you can keep your overhead really low. You pay only for what you need, when you need it; you don't have to worry about keeping someone on staff or paying a retainer. **There are entrepreneurs who are running fairly large enterprises singlehandedly, using outsourcing to handle their needs.** Again, they're only paying for what they need as they need it, so the overhead stays relatively low.

Speaking of outsourcing: I have a love and hate relationship with the Internet. To me, it represents the best of the best and the worst of the worst when it comes to marketing. **However, when it comes to finding all kinds of very specialized suppliers willing to take on a wide variety of tasks for competitive prices, you can't beat it.** It's the greatest invention ever for doing that, especially since a lot of the work is done overseas now. It helps you achieve all kinds of things for your customers that wouldn't have been easily possible before.

We're up to our seventh "done for you" program now, and we've incorporated this concept in other programs as well—like our new Cash in 48 Hours program, which I'm going to discuss in more detail later. **We've aggressively followed this approach because it's what our customers want. They want the results without the risks. They want the benefits without the effort. They want experts to take care of everything for them.** And so we take all the difficult, expensive, time-consuming, frustrating, high-risk aspects of the businesses onto our shoulders, so our clients can enjoy the benefits. **Basically, our clients become joint venture business partners with us.** We're structuring these things in a variety of ways, always coming up with new facets to try. We keep testing them and tweaking them, looking for ways to improve them. **This processes works best with services, so we often create services around existing business opportunities.** For example, we'll take a Network Marketing company and build our own proprietary marketing system around that company; and then, on top of that, we'll offer to do everything for our distributors or partners. They just can't get enough of it!

So join us! Come on in, the water's fine! **There's plenty of room for everybody here, because again, this principle does transcend markets.** For example: a minister friend recently turned me on to a website called Startachurch.com, and I just love what the lawyer who runs it is doing. His idea is so fascinating that I got myself onto his mailing list—so now I've been getting these emails for something I normally have no interest in. But this fellow is a tremendous marketer, and he offers his various services and information products for two prices: one where he just sells you the information and you can do it all yourself, and the other where he does everything for you.

Even though I don't know this guy and will probably never meet him, I'll bet you anything that 7 or 8 out of 10 of his customers choose the "done for you" service. People already have enough problems in their lives. They're frustrated, they're confused, they're overwhelmed, and this gives them the perfect alternative they're looking for. It's a sign of the times. **"Done for you" is a growing trend**—from the most basic kinds of things you can call your local repairperson for, all the way up to elaborate programs like the advertising and management services we offer or this lawyer's "Start a Church" idea.

People love these services, because they don't have the time or knowledge to do the work properly themselves. This factor applies even at the most basic scale of household needs, not just more esoteric things like business management. Here's a true story, courtesy of Chris Lakey. On a recent weekend, he was watching TV while a good-sized thunderstorm was moving through. Suddenly, a big lightning bolt struck close to his house; the electricity flickered, and the TV turned off. He had no idea what was going on, so he did what he always does in those situations: he tried to turn the TV back on, and nothing happened. Next he went to the entertainment system, where his TV, DVR, PS3, stereo, and similar components were located, and noticed that everything was off. And yet the power was on; it had only flickered. There was no indication that anything was wrong, except that none of those components were working.

So he looked behind the entertainment system and noticed

that his surge protector was also off. After testing the surge protector, Chris came to the conclusion that something must have happened to the electrical outlet. He noticed that something plugged in across the room in one of the other outlets was working, so he thought, *Well, maybe a breaker blew*. So he checked the breaker box, and found that all the outlets in the room were tied into the same breaker, so he assumed it wasn't the breaker—that something wasn't right with that one electrical outlet. So he ran an extension cord and plugged all the entertainment system components into another outlet in that room, and everything came back on, working fine. He was certain, then, that the outlet was out.

This happened on Friday night, so on Saturday Chris went to the hardware store and asked about replacing that outlet, and they pointed him to the right area. He discovered that the new outlet he needed to replace the fried one cost just 59 cents. So for about $1.20, he got two outlets. Now, he hasn't replaced the fried one yet because he's a little nervous about doing so, and he's no electrician; he plans to call one in and have him do it. This is great example of why "done for you" is so powerful. The part required to fix the electrical outlet cost 59 cents... and yet, Chris is tempted to pay someone else at least hundred times that amount to replace it. Admittedly, there's some risk involved; electricity is nasty stuff. But there's that part of him that goes, "Wow, I just paid 59 cents for this part, and I'm probably going to pay a hundred bucks to have an electrician come out and install it..." So he may still end up doing it himself, after all; he thinks he can manage it without electrocuting himself.

Chris also has a deck that needs to be stained. He *could* do it himself, he says, but he's definitely calling someone else out to do it. He also needs to repaint his living room... but he's going to use someone else, because it has high, vaulted ceilings, especially over the staircase, and he doesn't want to deal with having to buy a really tall ladder and all the other hassles that come with it. And he hates painting, anyway!

Those are just a few everyday examples of how the "done for you" mentality arises in real life. That segment of any industry is always going be highly profitable. These days, more and more people just want someone who's an expert to take care of whatever's gone wrong. **They want to know that someone else will do everything for them, and do a good job of it—and that they don't have to worry about it.** I think you'll see this playing out in your own life and experiences, if you think about it. There are probably plenty of things that you just don't want to do. It may be that you *can* do them, but you'd rather let someone else take care of it for you. Perhaps you don't mow your own yard or you don't trim your own trees, for example; something simple like that.

In any aspect of life that you can think of, there are undoubtedly people providing that service on a "done for you" basis, profiting by filling a need felt by people who don't want to do it themselves for whatever reason. The reason they don't want to do it isn't important; what matters is that they don't. **There's a gap in many marketplaces that can be filled by offering to do what people don't want to do on their own, but still want done.**

Earlier, I mentioned our Cash in 48 Hours system. We have an advertising service based on what we've now proven that our customers want—and that's where the profits lie in any business. **What matters isn't necessarily what *you* want; it's what *they* want.** We've found that many of our clients would like a hand-up, a little assistance, so we've found it very profitable to offer "done for you" advertising packages and options for them. Suppose you were looking for a way to advertise, and you approached a local ad agency. They could help you get your ads placed and you might say, "I want national exposure," and then they would buy ad space all over the U.S. in various media. Well, we offer that; but we also offer back-end services and management as well.

Let me explain how that works. Let's say you run a big national ad campaign, and you've got this toll-free hotline for all the leads to come in on. What happens when it does really well, and you're flooded with calls? Usually, it's up to you to convert the leads to sales and do all the customer service work; but we offer to do all that for our clients. **In essence, we've become a full-service advertising and management company. A big part of our business, in fact, is helping clients do all these things under one umbrella.** It's been an extremely successful campaign for us. We've struck a chord with our clients and with our broader marketplace, now that we've discovered that they really want these things done for them. Now, could our clients do all of the above on their own? Of course. In fact, some do. They may choose to advertise other ways, for example. But we offer these services so that people can have another option, so they can choose to have us take care of everything for them.

So give some serious thought to "done for you" services

in light of some of the things you experience and do on a regular basis. I think you'll start to see more and more ways that "done for you" is offered in the market at large. Consider retirement accounts. You know, you can manage your own retirement fund; you don't need a broker, though you might need some way of getting onto the trading floor. Essentially, you need a firm to buy and sell through, but you can manage that easily enough: There are all kinds of online brokerage firms available. Still, a lot of people like to have someone take care of their accounts for them. Similarly, there are all kinds of things being done in our society at large that illustrate this principle of "done for you" services.

I think you would be remiss if you didn't find a way to incorporate "done for you" into your business model; and I believe that there are enough examples available across all kinds of industries that there's no excuse not to. **No matter what you sell, no matter who you sell to, there are things you can do for those people that they probably don't want to do themselves, and might not even know *how* to do themselves.** If you add "do it for you" services, products, and opportunities to your mix, you'll see your sales and your profits increase as more people look for ways to get out of that work themselves.

Again, for this to work, **you'll first need to show people that you're an expert**—because they want to know they're working with somebody who knows what they're doing, knows what they're talking about, and can back up what they're saying. **These days, one of the easiest ways to establish that proof is to offer an information product—for example, a report or web video—in which you show people what needs**

to be done and tell them how they could do it themselves. By doing that, you prove that you're the expert, and then you can offer your service: your easy, no-risk way of doing it for them.

It may seem odd to give them all the knowledge and information they need to do the task, and then expect them to take you up on the offer; but many people will do just that. Admittedly, some people won't; when Chris was dealing with his electrical outlet problem, he went online and watched a little video of someone else changing theirs out on the free website Ehow.com, and now he feels pretty confident that he can do it on his own and save the electrician's fee. But he also tells me that there are plenty of times when he's watched a video on how to do something, and then decided to hire somebody else to do it for him anyway—because he felt like he just didn't want to tackle it.

So show them how to do it themselves first. Give them that option, and then offer them your service. And consider this: **because you're doing it for them, you can charge a premium price, which is one reason "done for you" can be a huge boost to your business model.** In this fast-changing world, we're looking for people we can trust, people we can depend on; and once we find somebody like that, why would we want to do a task ourselves? **Just prove to people that you're trustworthy and that you can do what you say, and you can make a fortune by taking care of everything for them.**

CHAPTER EIGHT

All this talk about retirement is nonsense! Work gives our lives purpose, meaning, and structure. Stop telling me to take it easy… ***I'll have eternity to take it easy!***

Forget Retirement!

All this talk about retirement is nonsense: **work gives our life meaning and purpose and structure.** So please: stop telling me to take it easy, because I'll have eternity to take it easy! I'll take easy when I die. Until then I want to move! I want to live! I want to challenge myself! I want to go for it!

I firmly believe that retirement sucks, and that it's a bad idea for most people. **Now, I do think that some people are able to retire *towards* something—that they can have a full life beyond the work that they do, as long as they get involved in other things after retirement.** But too many people are like my father. I watched him die far too soon, and I attribute that partly to the fact that he retired. When he was working, he was active, constantly involved in things. He had a full schedule. He had lots of things going on, the phone was always ringing, there was always a demand for his time, he was working with people he enjoyed working with, life was full, and he was contributing. He was good at what he did; he enjoyed his job and he enjoyed the people he worked with. He was busy and active and excited!

Then, when he retired, all those people he was working with... well, their lives didn't change one iota. He's the one who stepped out of the stream; the river kept moving, and it wasn't moving with him in it anymore, so he was left behind.

The phone stopped ringing. Pretty soon he had nothing to do, and he didn't have it within himself to try to get some other gig going. **He was a good man, a very intelligent man, but he spent way too much time after retirement just doing nothing.** Laziness overtook him; he had his favorite chair, and he spent a lot of time sitting in it. He spent a lot of time eating while he was sitting in that chair, and he spent a lot of time watching TV. **When he was working, he was happy; and when he quit working, he just started declining.**

Work is good for you. Khalil Gibran, the famous poet, wrote, **"Work is love made visible."** I've always liked that quote. **There's nothing like being excited about what you do and the people you work with, and having various projects going on so that you're always excited about something.** You're reaching for something, your reach is always exceeding your grasp, and you're moving forward. You've got things you're looking forward to, you're hoping for, and projects you're excited about. That's what life is, and work is just a great outlet for all of that. It gives structure and meaning to your life. Oh, it's not the only thing that does; some people are able to retire from work and actually lead full, rich lives thereafter. **But for most people, work provides the structure they can't provide for themselves—which is why I think that retirement is a terrible idea.**

My dear, sweet Mom is 78 years old, and she still works. Last summer, I asked her, "Mom, when are you planning on retiring?" She said, "Oh, in about 10 years," and I loved that! She just melted my heart! All my siblings tell me that my Mom is working too hard; I hear it from them all the time. But I don't buy it at all. Yeah, she's tired sometimes—no question about it. **But she's doing the kind of work she enjoys; it's stimulating to her.** She's doing work she's good at doing, and even though she's 78 years old, she damn sure doesn't look like most 78 year olds. **She has lots of energy and passion and enthusiasm for life.** She's just not sitting around all day. She's out there moving and shaking and making things happen!

We've all heard the old saying, "a rolling stone gathers no moss." That quote must be at least 500 years old, probably older. And it's just as true now as when it was first coined. **When people are idle too much of the time, and lack enough structure in their lives, they turn soft and flabby...** and I'm not just talking about physically. They do so in all aspects, including mentally.

You know, a lot of people claim that they just want to make a lot of money in their business ventures; but I think what people *really* want is something to get excited about. **They want something that makes them feel young again; something that keeps them moving, that challenges them.** Those are all the things that you can get through work. So I say "Yes!" to work and self-employment and entrepreneurship, and refusing to buy into this whole governmental retirement program. Retirement just isn't a good idea. Stay active! Find something you're passionate about! **Find work that gets you excited and gives you something to look forward to all the time.** That's what work is to me.

I've held this belief since I was quite young, and so has my Marketing Director, Chris Lakey. He's 36 right now—over halfway to what most people would consider retirement age. **But**

he's never really planned on retiring in the traditional sense. He says that when he first actively talked to people about that, they acted like he was some kind of madman. "How could you *not* plan on retiring? How could you *not* invest for this day when you turn 65 and stop working?" The truth is, investing has been more of a personal preference than a retirement strategy to Chris.

I think that a lot of people get stuck in the mindset that, well, you go to work when you're 18 and you work all those years, and when you turn 65 you retire and get the gold watch from the company—and you ride off into the sunset in a RV, and live off the retirement investments you've made. Well, thank goodness I didn't go that route—and it's especially a good thing that I didn't turn 65 in the last couple of years. I would imagine there are a lot of people who planned on retiring in the last few years whose savings and investment accounts were wiped out by this horrible economy we're mired in. Some of the big investment companies have gone under, and a lot of the surviving funds have lost so much value that they're currently worth very little. Not to mention the fact that we've been printing so much money in the last couple of years that the value of the dollar is worth quite a bit less than it was just a few years ago. **What this all adds up to is the fact that for many, the dream of building a big nest egg for retirement is more of a nice idea than a reality that's actually transpired.**

In general, I think the problem is that people have this feeling that work is a four-letter word, and so they want to do as little of it as possible. Therefore, as soon as they're able, they're going to stop working and start doing something they love, something that excites them. They spend all their lives doing things they don't enjoy and don't get passion out of, and they hate it. **Well, there are all kinds of opportunities for you to do what you love and make money doing it.** And maybe, in some way, that just means learning to love what you're already doing, not necessarily finding something that you love and then doing it. There's a certain truth in finding passion or enjoyment in whatever you're stuck with, if that's the way it is.

I think that having a purpose, having something you're working toward, drives you to health and happiness. When you give that up, that's when you cease to exist, in a sense; and that may ultimately mean your death. Death can happen long before your physical body dies, if you just give up on your passions and become sedentary, existing without real purpose. That's why I tell people, "Stop telling me to take it easy. I have eternity to take it easy! I'll take it easy when I'm dead!"

This reminds me of a scene in the Disney movie *Up!*, which progresses really fast at the beginning. The main character starts as a kid; and within several minutes of the movie starting, he's an old man, and his house is being surrounded by construction, and they're trying to take his house (through eminent domain, of course). He doesn't want to give it up, and one of the guys is there and he's talking to him about taking his house and how the boss is going to increase the offer. The main character tells them, "You can have my house," and the other guy perks up. "What?" And the old guy says, "When I'm dead!" The point is, there's all kinds of time to take it easy later—when you're gone. **In the meantime, you can work, and find passion and purpose and meaning in the work that you do, and you can live a long, healthy, and enjoyable life well past**

the "retirement" years.

Those are some of the things I think about when I think about retirement, which I equate with stopping. Usually, stopping isn't a good thing: so keep moving and enjoying life long past whatever age the government tells you is retirement age. **According to Zig Ziglar, the whole idea of retiring when you're 65 years old only originated 150-170 years ago in Germany.** There was a new politician coming into office, and he wanted to get rid of all of the people who remained from an earlier administration; so he just made a law setting the mandatory retirement age at 65. That cleared out most of the people he wanted to get rid of. It makes sense that some kind of bureaucrat would invent something like that, and the law was never changed.

You know, it's funny how the retirement law, as it stands today, say you have to retire at a certain age, or you don't get all this money you've been working toward. But then, if you wait five years, you can go back to work again and still collect all your benefits. Why did they arrange it that way? **Because most people die between retirement and the time they can go back to work and still receive all their benefits.** I honestly believe that for most people, retirement equals death; and so I hope you'll give that some sincere, serious thought.

I truly believe my Dad died way before his time—and I watched my stepdad die too young, too, simply because he was retired and not staying active enough. **Work will keep you active.**

Chapter Nine

**In business,
if you rest,
<u>you rust</u>.**

Don't Let Yourself Rust!

In business, if you rest, you rust.

My favorite metaphor for business is that it's like riding a bike up a hill: The minute you stop pedaling, you fall down. **And so many people in business do stop pedaling once they achieve some success; they decide to coast, and quit doing the things that got them there to begin with.** They rest a little too much, and suddenly they stop getting the results that they used to get when they were pedaling like mad.

You've got to keep moving in business. The market is always changing, so *you've* got to change in order to keep up with your market.

Here at M.O.R.E., Inc., we're currently re-writing a bunch of our old promotions. In particular, I'm working on one that we did eight years ago. I worked through the past weekend on it, and I was laughing to my wife about all the changes I had to make, even for something we created back in 2003. I don't want to go into all the specifics, but we were saying things eight years ago that we don't say anymore—because the market has changed, just in that relatively brief period of time.

In business, you have to keep learning and growing if you expect to succeed long-term. **You're got to keep that ear to the ground and constantly test new things.** We're doing a test right now that, if it holds true, is going to violate so much of what used to work for us... But it's also going to prove to us just how different the world is now, and it's going to open up some exciting new doors, because it's a great money-saving idea. As a promotion, we're going to be able to make little postcards work in conjunction with a 17-minute Internet movie that Chris Lakey put together. If it works for us, as opposed to our traditional two-step marketing model, then that's going to pioneer an exciting new model. Eventually, we'll test a 37-minute movie or a 47-minute movie, or we'll test a giant postcard. **We'll test, test, test!**

We have to, because everything is always changing. Success is a moving target. **By testing lots of different things and constantly experimenting, by keeping your eyes and ears open, you'll continue to grow.** You'll learn new things, and you'll maintain your competitive advantage. Part of the reason why you have to do all that is because new, hungrier, smarter, more aggressive, more ruthless competitors are nipping at your heels all the time. **Oftentimes it happens that entrepreneurs build very successful businesses, only to lose those businesses because they get conservative, complacent, or lazy.** They're unwilling to do what they did before, and so they lose their edge, their hunger. **That's when these young guns come in there and kick their asses.** It happens so often it's almost a cliché. So fair warning, for those of you who want to maintain your edge.

Admittedly, it's not easy to do so. But then again, to me, "easy" represents boring. As I mentioned earlier, I intend to take it easy when I die. I'll have eternity to take it easy. In the meantime I want to live, I want to grow, I want to challenge myself, I want to move! Business is not supposed to be easy.

Anything that's too easy is boring, at least to me, and I can't stand being bored. I hate that worse than anything. I'd rather put up with the pain of the never-ending struggle of riding that bike up the hill. I'd much rather deal with that than deal with smooth sailing or, worse, having too much time on my hands. I prefer dealing with problems; or better yet, call them challenges.

The only real difference between a problem and a challenge is this: a problem is something that you don't want to do, or that you're looking at in a negative way. A challenge is that same situation, but it's something you're excited about tackling and overcoming. It stimulates you rather than tearing you down or breaking you apart. It actually makes you stronger. It's something that you *want* to overcome.

It's a cliché that people do tend to become more complacent and conservative as they age. They get older and softer, losing the competitive edge they used to have. **This is a case where success is not necessarily a good thing, because it can lull people to sleep.** There's a story (and I'm sure there's some truth to it) about how scientists have experimented with putting frogs in hot water. If they dump the frogs in the hot water right away, the frogs freak out and jump out really fast. But if they put the frogs in lukewarm water, the frogs just float there calmly. If the experimenters then start heating the water very slowly, the frogs acclimate to the increased warmth; they relax and accept it, and pretty soon, unless the scientist rescues those frogs, they'll boil in that water and die. They won't even try to get out.

I think about that story all the time in relation to success, because I think that success can be like that boiling water.

Success is the one thing we're all after. Who doesn't want success? But then you get some, and you're like that frog floating in the lukewarm water; everything is nice and it all feels so good. Pretty soon that water starts heating up, and you can't respond quickly enough to get out—you've become complacent and slow, and you lose what success you've acquired. Now, this may not be the perfect analogy, **but my point is that you need to be very careful of anything that lulls you to sleep.** Any time you start pining for an easier business, and wishing that the struggle weren't so hard, and come to hate all of the problems within your business—that's when the red flags should go up.

In the business arena, it's your competitors who are putting you in the hot water—or maybe not so much your competitors as much as the market forces. **It's too easy to get to a place where you feel too comfortable, and fail to jump, especially if the change is gradual.** Oh sure, if the water starts out too hot, you immediately react to it. But if the water is nice and warm, it may lull you into complacency. You get used to the way things are going and won't ever stop to realize you're in a pot of hot water, and pretty soon you get boiled alive (in the metaphorical sense). **As an entrepreneur, that means your marketplace passes you by.** Your methods are outdated, or your ideas are stale. Perhaps you're using old technology, simply not keeping up with the times.

Today, that might mean staying offline while your competitors are profitably leveraging the Internet; or maybe your competitors have found ways to use social media that you're not taking advantage of. Now, depending on your industry, I think some businesses can do well enough without those media. But it may be that you're hindered by your unwillingness to get involved in Twitter or Facebook or YouTube when all your competitors have. You become outdated. **Your customers pass you by in favor of these newer forms of receiving information, products, and services, and you're left dying on the vine.** I think a lot of entrepreneurs suffer from that, because they're not continuing their educations. I'm not talking about formal education; they're simply not learning. They're not seeking new knowledge, not staying in tune with their marketplace. **Markets change, and shift, and new developments occur constantly; if you're not actively staying on top of all that, you risk losing your competitive edge.**

Consider a start-up company that's got just a few employees, or maybe just one entrepreneur behind it. Let's say it's a successful company: it grows, it builds, it expands, and before you know it, it's had its IPO and it's a public company. Now it's got millions of shareholders from all over the country, and they've got a Board, and pretty soon the entrepreneur who started the company doesn't really run the company anymore. The Board makes all the decisions. Even though he or she cashed out and had a nice payday, the entrepreneur no longer has much creative control... and so the company becomes lethargic, loses its youthful energy, and there's no real spark there anymore. They just drudge through the days and do what they do; they pay dividends to the shareholders, and there's no new innovation. **Think of Apple Computers before Steve Jobs came back in the 1990s. That's what you risk with resting.**

This principle applies to businesses of all size, even small mom-and-pop businesses. In fact, it probably applies even more so to businesses of that type or size. **If you're not on top of your industry, ensuring that you continue to know more about your marketplace that anyone else, if you're not actively trying to take your game to the next level, you *will* be left behind.** It's only a matter of time. There's no opportunity, really, to stand still in business; this concept of resting and rusting, I think, is an appropriate analogy. **If you leave something sitting still for too long it will rust or corrode.** If you reach for it six months or a year later, it's not going to be in as good a shape as it might be if you used it every day and took good care of it. Try leaving a computer sitting still. Let's say you walk away from your computer and go back to it a year later. Unless you've taken care of it, it will have collected dust, and you'll have issues with it just because it has aged, sitting there unused.

The entrepreneur who stays in motion is going to be free from rust and is going to stay on top of his or her game. If you keep striving, you'll be at an advantage over your competitors who don't. So motion is good. Progress is good. Resting, or sitting still, or taking it easy… all these things are metaphors for ultimate failure in business, I think.

At the time of this recording, I'm 52 years old—and I'm thinking about things at 52 that I didn't think about at 42, I can tell you that. I see that the window of life is closing, and I can see it closing faster than ever before. As I was telling my wife over the weekend, there's not a lot of good that comes from getting older. I mean, the body starts falling apart and you deal with all these aches and pains. None of that is going to get any better; I know that! **But the one thing we all have to look**

forward to in business, as long as we make a decision to keep active, is that we can continue to get better and better.

Challenges don't have to be negative. **The experience adds up, the knowledge and wisdom develops, and through all of that, the work is exciting.** It gives you something to hope for and something to reach for and get energized about. So keep that in mind. Keep that in your focus.

Chapter Ten

**Does talent create its own opportunities?
Or does your total passion and commitment to
the opportunities create its own talent?**

Talent vs Opportunity

Does talent create its own opportunities, or does passion and commitment to opportunities create its own talent?

That's not just a word play, or an exercise in semantics. It's a dichotomy, if you will, that lies at the heart of any business effort. **What contributes most to success: talent, or commitment?** Many people think that you have to be born with a certain amount of talent to succeed at anything. There's an old saying that goes, "Talent rises," meaning that if you're born with a lot of talent at something, you'll eventually go straight to the top. I'll admit that talent can, in fact, be important; and yet there are millions and perhaps hundreds of millions, perhaps even *billions* of people who, like myself, weren't born with any kind of real talent. **Whatever talent I have today, I've had to work for; and I'm only good at a few things.** But I'm constantly honing my skills, and I'm getting better at those things all the time—and I got there because of this concept here.

I've been totally passionate about these things! **I've been totally committed to doing the best I can in these areas, and improving my abilities as time passes.** If I'm lucky enough to live for another decade or two, I'll become even more talented in these areas, because I'll keep pushing. But the honest truth is that any talent I may have didn't come freely; it had to be earned.

I do agree that talent does rise, but I'm also a firm believer that you create your own talent. **It's your desire that truly matters: how badly you really want to do something, and the total focus that you apply to it.** You really have to dedicate yourself. You have to become very hungry, so to speak, in order to force yourself to put in the time and effort necessary to develop and hone that talent. **It takes a serious level of self-discipline to decide that you're going to stick with something and refuse to give up.** You have to vow that you're not going to quit, no matter what!

Desire, focus, discipline, and determination: those are the things that ultimately create the talent or skills necessary for you to rise to the top. Very often, you create your own talent. I firmly believe that.

Admittedly, this philosophy goes against the grain of traditional thinking. **And it remains largely a secret because when they don't immediately succeed (at least in a small way) at whatever they're trying to do, most people just say, "Oh well, I don't have the talent for this," and just give up on it.** I've seen this with my own granddaughter, Ashley. When the grandkids come over, most of them like to play with my drum set; and so I was trying to encourage Ashley to learn to play the drums. This is maybe four years ago, and she told me, "Oh, Grandpa, I have no talent for that." So I told her, "Honey, you create your own talent," and she just looked at me like I was speaking some foreign language. I was surprised that a young girl would think that way, frankly, but it's all too common.

Stop thinking that you're not good enough. **You can *become* good at anything, if you try hard enough.** Let me just give you few examples of things that I'm personally trying to develop my talent in. The item at the top of my list is public speaking. As I mentioned in an earlier Way, I've always enjoyed a good public speaker—somebody who can get up in front of the crowd and move the audience emotionally, who can get them excited and fired up. Whenever I've seen a public speaker do that, I've always thought, *Man, how cool is that to do?!*

About 10 or 15 years ago I started paying attention to the best public speakers in a different way; instead of saying, "Oh, I'll never be able to do that," I said to myself, "I want to be able to do that!" The problem was, I was absolutely, positively terrified to speak in public. And yet I *wanted* to do it. **So I taught myself to get up in front of crowds and speak. It took me about a decade to become anything that would even remotely resemble being comfortable up there.**

Certainly, I'm *never* comfortable in the very beginning; but as I proceed, I warm up, getting very comfortable with being up front. I really like it. In fact, as my friend Russ von Hoelscher says, once I get started, you can't shut me up! But this has never, ever come naturally to me. I had to consciously decide to try to emulate all those speakers that I thought were so cool. Am I there yet, even after all this time? Hardly. I'm still teaching myself how to do it, and I don't claim to be a great public speaker; **I'm just trying to be as good as *I* can be. But the point is that I've taught myself how to speak in front of groups because I had a strong desire to do so, despite my lack of obvious talent—instead of just giving up when my talent didn't "rise" to the occasion.**

Another area I'm trying to get really good at is copywriting—writing advertisements and sales messages that get people all jazzed up, causing them to take some kind of an action to develop and strengthen the relationships that I have with them. **I've been working on this for more than 20 years.** Now, I've always wanted to be a writer. When I was a teenager I used to write poetry. In fact, I thought I was a great poet; I used to write poems for the girls, but it never went much farther than that. Later, when I saw Russ von Hoelscher write some of our early sales letters, I thought, *Man, how cool is that!* You know the story: We'd pay Russ a few thousand dollars to come over on the weekends and work with us. We'd talk about all these ideas for products, services, and opportunities that we could promote to our customers, and then Russ would get all excited and start writing sales copy longhand on the legal pads we provided for him. After he left on Sunday, we'd take those legal pads over to the typist, she would type everything up, and then we would turn them into sales letters and send them out—and people would send us their money. I wanted to emulate Russ so badly! The problem was that despite wanting to be a writer for so long, I wasn't any good, really. In fact, I kind of sucked as a writer. Even after over two decades of writing on a daily basis and really trying as hard as I can, I'm probably just barely good enough as it is. ***But I am good enough.*** Whatever talent I've had, I've had to work for it… and I'm still working for it.

Remember, it's the desire! The focus! The discipline! The determination! Those are the things that truly matter here.

I've got a new goal that I set almost six months ago, because I want to be the very best copywriter that I can possibly be. **I set a goal to write at least 100,000 words every single month.** That's basically the equivalent of a normal-sized book—

over 300 pages. One hundred thousand words a month breaks down to about 3,600 words every day. I try to shoot for 4,000, no matter what. We've got a seminar coming up this week and I'm going to be gone for four days, but I'm still going to try to get my 4,000 words written every single day for that entire period. I'm going to have my laptop computer with me. I'm going to be in the back of the room writing as I'm listening to the presenters up on stage. I'm going to be writing at nighttime and in the early morning hours in my hotel room. **Why? Because I want to become the best I can be!** It's just as simple as that.

Realize that in many ways, "talent" is a synonym for "skill." **A lot of what we call talent is really very hard work combined with experience, with the lessons learned internalized so that the skills become automatic.** I believe it's better for you to cut the word "talent" from your vocabulary. Just get rid of it altogether and replace it with the word "skill"—because a skill is something you can develop, whereas a talent is something that people think you have to be born with. **You develop your own skills.** You have to want something bad enough, you have to set some goals, and you have to push yourself. **But here's an interesting fact: the more you want something, the less it becomes like work.** Oh, it may still be difficult to do; believe me, when I get up to do my 4,000 words every morning, it's not easy. Some mornings it's easier than others, sure—but some mornings, it's very, very difficult. It always requires a certain amount of discipline, and I have to rework my whole schedule sometimes just to make that goal every day. But I want to become the best copywriter I can be, so I'm willing to make the sacrifices.

A third area where I'm continually honing my skills is business in general. In my opinion, I still suck at being an entrepreneur, so it's something I'm trying to get better at all the time. Recently, I was joking with someone about how little I used to know, and how little I still know to this day; my humor tends to be the self-deprecating kind. There's some truth to that joke, but the thing is, **you can't let a little thing like the fact that you're not that good at something stop you.** I never let it stop me! Seriously, I wasn't born with any special abilities. I think that, in some ways, those people who are born with strong gifts are as cursed as they are blessed. Their gifts can cause them so much pain.

I think if I had a choice of being who I am today—someone who wasn't blessed with a high IQ, with no special abilities or talents, so that I'd have to work my ass off every day just to be able to perform at the level I wanted to perform—versus being some super-talented person who just skates through life and never has to really exert himself, then I would choose the former every time. **I see very talented people every day who just squander their talents.**

So think about that, and consider the question I posed at the beginning of this way: Does talent create opportunities, or do you create opportunities and then develop the necessary talent? Which comes first, the chicken or the egg? It's hard to say. We've all heard about child prodigies and other people who just seem to have inborn talent for certain things. You might see someone who's an exceptional athlete or musician, and hear people talking about how they were born with it, or how they somehow don't have to work hard for what they've got.

I think of childhood athletes like Tiger Woods, for example; there are videos of him as a little two or three-year-old out there on the golf course, hitting balls further than a lot of adults can hit them. Now, that may be a stretch, but you get the point. Or you hear about a childhood musician who can play the piano like a virtuoso. Mozart was like that... and some kids today can play the piano as well as he did. We like to think that somehow, this just happens magically—that some people have a talent, and other people don't. And if you have it, then, well good for you: you're going to have a long career in that particular field, and you're going to make lots of money and I'm going to be jealous my whole life, because I wasn't born with it and you were! Boo hoo, woe is me, etc., etc.

And the reality is that, yes, some people do have natural talents. But that's not true for most people. On the contrary, many people have to work extremely hard for their successes in their chosen fields. They become committed to success at any cost, and refuse to give up, and so they achieve the success that they were looking for. Even so-called natural talents like Tiger Woods often work hard for years and years before they really succeed. Look at the Williams sisters in tennis, Serena and Venus. They may be amazingly talented, but like Woods, they worked very, very hard from childhood on to nurture those talents, refusing to give up until they were at the very top of their field. And they still have to fight to keep from being unseated by new challengers!

Talented or not, in order to truly succeed at anything, you require total passion and commitment to the opportunities that help create the talent. You have to put yourself into a situation to maximize your opportunity for success. This requires an unswerving dedication to honing your skills every single day. If you're just okay at something—you're not excellent at it, you don't excel at it, but you do okay at it—you can still achieve a certain level of success if you work at it with drive and dedication.

Chris Lakey's 14-year-old daughter is learning to play the guitar. She's only played the acoustic guitar so far, and right now she can only play chords, and doesn't read music. She's just learned it in the last year, because it was available to her and she decided it was something she'd like to do because she likes to sing. She likes to write music too, and so she picked that up, and decided to take a class at school. So she's learned the basics now. But does she have any raw talent at playing guitar? That's still up in the air. Now, Chris' family is musically inclined, and she does have a beautiful singing voice that could, maybe, be attributed to Chris' genes. But neither he nor his wife play guitar; she learned that all on her own.

At this point, one of two things can happen: she can stick where she is, or she can work at it until she gets better and masters her guitar-playing skills. I fear that unless she does decide to take it to the next level, she's going to plateau—she'll be able to play what she can play now, and that's about it. Oh, she might get a little better at it; she might even learn to play whatever songs you can play in those chords. But that will be about the extent of it, because even if she can play those fairly well with practice, she'll never learn anything new.

That's one option. I imagine a lot of adults are like that. They might know a little bit about whatever instrument they played when they were younger, and maybe they can still play a little bit today, but they've certainly never excelled at it. **They've never taken their ability to the next level.** So one of two things will happen for her and her acoustic guitar playing skills.

The other option is that she continues to have a passion for learning the acoustic guitar, and she'll continue to try to pick up new things; and a few years from now, she'll be a lot better. Maybe five or 10 years from now she'll be even better still, and perhaps she'll be writing full songs and be performing somewhere. Who knows what the future holds for her? She's just a 14-year-old! But the point is, she has an opportunity right now to decide if she's going to have a passion and a commitment to learn to play the guitar... or whether she's going to let that go by the wayside.

Is doing well in business a talent? That's hard to say. Let's assume that you've detected a little raw talent for business in yourself, though. So what do you do with it? How do you develop it, and spin it into business success? **You could approach business success from an educational perspective: if talent isn't necessarily needed, then maybe you can teach yourself to succeed in business by getting yourself a business degree.** And so, you do your time and pay your money, and you emerge four years later with a diploma in hand. Maybe that would enhance or even replace raw talent, because now you have the head knowledge you need to succeed. Is that enough? Maybe… maybe not.

The opposite of that would be a scenario in which you see other people succeed, you know the details of their success, and their success makes you realize that it's possible for you to be successful too. You approach business with verve and passion, and a commitment to taking on good opportunities and learning what it takes to make money. **You study the success stories you observed in the first place, you follow those people around, and you model what you do after what they do.** Eventually, through determination and drive, you become successful in business.

Those two methods contrast fairly sharply—and **I honestly think that there are many more opportunities available to people who follow the second path than for those who follow the first. If you rely on your own raw talent or education, you can only get so far.** And sure, there are people who ride raw talent to varying degrees of success. For example, certain athletes come from athletic families. The son of an NFL player might have the physical attributes and inborn skills to become an NFL athlete—although very few children of NFL players also go on to have NFL careers, so clearly, it's not all about just being born with it. It does happen, though, in just about any field: business, sports, music, or whatever. So that's one path to success. But more often than not, the path that you see the ultra-successful take is the one that harnessed the desire and the passion and the commitment to succeed to create the talent necessary to be successful. These are the people, for example, who put in long hours at the gym to become successful athletes.

As I'm writing this, the NFL season is just getting underway. I recently spoke to somebody about how physical conditioning, as a condition of being on the team, is almost a given these days. You don't go to training camp expecting to get into shape; no, you come to training camp *already* in shape, because you're dedicated to being a wide receiver or an offensive lineman or quarterback or whatever your position is. You've put in the time in the gym, you've lifted weights, and you're in the best shape of your life—because you know you have to be. Someone who comes to training camp 20 pounds overweight and out of shape isn't going to have a job for long, unless they're a star player… in which case they probably wouldn't be in that condition anyway.

Top athletes are dedicated to doing whatever it takes to reach and stay in their positions, just as someone in business must be dedicated to the craft of being successful in business. **It doesn't matter what marketplace you're in or what your product lineup is like; if you intend to succeed, you can't play the game of business in a half-hearted manner.** You don't spend your days lollygagging around on the Internet or playing solitaire, while wishing customers would come in. You're out there hustling customers! You're out there visiting your competition and talking to people and doing things to improve on your business and marketing skills. Over time, you either improve your game as an entrepreneur... or you don't. If you do, you'll soon see the fruits of that effort: your business is growing, you're expanding, you're doing more sales than you've done before. **If you don't improve, you still get the fruits of your efforts, but they're bitter.** Your business starts to contract and will soon die, if you don't get out there and hustle.

Talent can create opportunities, but those opportunities are limited by all kinds of other factors. **Passion and commitment to creating your *own* talent will take you a lot farther, and it really is determined by your desire to continue down the path**

you've chosen. I truly do think that **gives you the ability to go farther than mere talent alone,** and I recommend it as the better path for you—one that will result in a more sustained success over a longer period of time. I think you'll see that if you study the outstanding successes in any marketplace or field. In fact, I heard once that if you just followed a successful person around for a few days, at the end of that time, you'd say, "Oh, no wonder they're successful!" But how many of us ever get a chance to do something like that? It's more likely that you'll encounter people who *aren't* successful in their endeavors... in which case, you should do the exact opposite of what they're doing.

Again, our beliefs do help create our reality. The belief that you have to be born with some special talent in order to succeed in any major way is fallacious, and will actually become a self-fulfilling prophecy—if you let it.

Chapter Eleven

Neatness rejects involvement. Dumb your sales letters down. ***Make them look homely.***

Dumb Your Sales Copy Down

On the face of it, the above headline may seem a bit insulting to your marketplace. But I don't mean it that way. **Earlier, I pointed out that people prefer to do business with other people just like them—not with people they perceive as being too slick and neat and perfect to be trusted.** In fact, that's one of the biggest secrets to our success here at M.O.R.E., Inc.: we're just ordinary people. **Well, one corollary to this concept is they don't want to see copywriting that comes across as too slick and neat and perfect.** This is certainly true of direct mail, but it can apply to other types of sales materials as well. Basically, it comes down to this: **Neatness rejects involvement.** Dumb your sales letters down. Make them look homely.

We've learned that the best sales letters are the ones that look real and raw. They look like a real person wrote them. Sometimes they're even kind of rough. Too many of the sales letters that I look at, especially from newcomers, are too neat and clean and pretty. From a graphic arts standpoint, they do look nice; but they're homogenized, bland, boring—and bored people don't buy! **Sales material gets boring very quickly if it's all in the same font, or if it's all nicely balanced and professional-looking.**

And that's the whole problem in a nutshell: people

think their sales material absolutely *has* to look professional, whatever the hell that means! They make an extra effort to give it a corporate look—but that can damage its effectiveness. Back in the early 1990s, I myself went through this phase where I started thinking, "Oh man, our sales material needs to look more professional." **I'll never forget how I took this one sales letter and made it look very pretty, and printed it on really nice paper; I was so proud of it,** because it projected precisely the kind of image I wanted to project. It was superbly professional! Well, I mailed it to our prospects—and nothing happened. **The sales were flat. I never did that again; lesson learned and taken to heart.**

Remember: if something looks too neat and clean and pretty and professional, it's boring. ***Bored people don't buy.* Excited people buy! Interested people buy!** So you've got to make your sales material look exciting and interesting. **One of the ways that we do that is by using hand marks, making it look like we've added this note here or that one there by hand.** The graphic artists don't like it, but we mark it up. We use different fonts and different sizes of fonts, and to make the pages of the sales letter look different, we use boxes and all kinds of weird stuff just to break things out.

Also, we write the copy in a natural style. Now, when I write copy, I write as fast as I can. You can always go back and edit and clean up later, and I do. **But I always keep this fact firmly in mind: People want to do business with other people like them.** So the more you can do to make your sales material look personable—to make them feel as if a real person wrote it, that it wasn't written by somebody talking down to them or by somebody using language that's just too neat and clean and pretty—the more successful you'll be. Write like a *real* person!

I wrote something that I'm a little proud of this morning: a five-page cover letter that the people coming to one of our seminars will receive when they check into their hotel, along with a big package of other material. **In the P.S. of the cover letter I wrote, "Right before your head hits the pillow, here's a bedtime story that can make you rich," and it was all about making money.** It was a story from my own life, a story we like to tell to set the stage and get people to thinking a certain way—to get them prepared for what they're about to undergo over the next few days.

I wonder how many marketers have ever written something like that to their clients? For all I know, I'm the only one. **The point is, it's different and fresh!** So much of the stuff out there is so homogenized that it's like the writers are afraid that they're going to offend somebody. They don't want to say anything off-color or use informal language. They opt for formal language instead, and it comes off as stiff and boring, because people don't speak that way. **Sales letters should be written the way you speak. The writing has to be natural;** it has to give a person the feeling that another person—preferably a person with a huge personality—wrote it. That's the kind of thing that *does* force involvement. **Neatness rejects involvement, whereas sounding real can pull people in and get them involved.** The very best copywriters in the world are the ones who can let their personality show through. I'll admit, it does take time to learn how to write at that level.

And when I recommend that you write as fast as you can

and then go back and clean it up, sometimes you don't want to clean it up too much. You just want it to be natural. You don't want it to sound stiff and polished. **You definitely don't want it to be "professional" or "corporate-looking" or any of that nonsense.** Stuff written that way just goes straight into the trash can!

I was talking to a marketer a few months ago, and they were asking me if I thought they should have a brochure done. Well, my whole attitude about brochures is that pretty much nobody reads them, that nobody gives a damn and they don't do any selling… period. I've seen only a few brochures that I thought did a good job of selling. **Most of them are full of that fluffy, professional, corporate nonsense that nobody cares about.** And all this talk about logos… that doesn't sell anything either!

So, is there such a thing as an image? Yes, of course there is. **But when it comes to people spending money, what they really want is to do business with other people who know their stuff, people who are experts, so that they can be confident that those people know what they're talking about.** But they also want a friendly relationship with somebody. If it's too stiff, too formal, too homogenized, too clean, they don't want anything to do with it. People like that aren't the best salespeople! The best salespeople are real, natural, normal. I've mentioned that old movie from the 1980s before, *Planes, Trains, and Automobiles*. Study John Candy's character in that movie. He was a happy-go-lucky kind of guy, a plain fellow with all his faults right out in view. Steve Martin's character was neat and clean and pretty and precise and professional. The contrast between those two men was very sharp. I think that when it comes to selling, the best salespeople are much more like John Candy than Steve Martin. They're "out there." Love 'em or hate 'em, at least you know you can *trust* them, because they're just themselves.

Many years ago, when I first became self-employed, I used to work the flea markets on the weekend. I got to know all the other flea market dealers, and while it was a lot of work, it was also a lot of fun. Well, the sellers who always made the most money didn't have neat, clean tables. They had stuff all over their tables, and people liked to rummage through it. Browsers were almost compelled to touch and dig and tear through all this stuff. It got people involved. **If something is too neat and clean and professional, you can just walk right by it.**

You want to get people involved, because that's one of the steps necessary in order to sell them. You've got to catch their attention and interest, because again, bored people don't buy. That's true in all kinds of selling situations. Think about the situations you've found yourself in as a buyer. Think about the times you've been in a store looking around, just killing some time, and a sales clerk came up and asked if he could help you with something. Your response is often, "I'm just looking," or something similar, because what you really want is for them to go away so you can keep browsing in your bored state. They can get on with helping somebody else and you can keep just doing what you're doing. You're not really intent on buying.

Suppose you happen to head over to another aisle and something catches your eye. You pick it up, and as you're handling it another sales clerk comes over and encourages you (with a little more energy than the last person) to take a good look and handle it as much as you like. Then he tells you about how he bought one of these himself, and how excited he is with this new toy, and how it will do all these neat things, and no home should be without one. **He gets you all excited, and the next thing you know you're walking out with one! Well, it's *because* you got excited. You were no longer in a bored state.** You were no longer just killing time. You became a prospect for this gadget that captured your imagination and got you all worked up.

It's the same thing with buying a car. No one goes in to buy a car and walks out with one that they were bored with during the buying process. People don't necessarily *like* to buy cars, but they do get excited about driving the car that they choose to buy. A salesperson who can keep the energy high and keep the prospect excited about that car is more likely to make the sale than someone who just goes through the motions. If you're bored and you're trying to buy a car, you're not as likely to walk out with a deal than if you feel like you have to have this car because you've been excited to think about yourself driving it, and you think about all the exciting things you're going to do with it. Maybe it's a sports car; or maybe you've never had a new car, and it's your first. Whatever the case may be, when you're excited, the **enthusiasm often translates into a sale.**

Earlier, I talked about the difference between an ugly sales letter and one that's more professional looking. **High-gloss sales letters are boring because they're too neat, and so it's easy to dismiss them.** They look like everything else, too, which is another problem with most advertising these days. There's nothing unique about it. The ads and commercials start to blend together, don't they? Especially on TV: they're all loud, obnoxious, and say the same things. There's nothing there to make you want to stop and pay attention.

Now, very occasionally I've seen a muted TV ad—but they're rare. Sometimes there's no talking at all. You're waiting for your favorite show to come back, suffering through the loud, blaring commercials where people are yelling and screaming at you—the commercials are always louder than the regular TV show anyway, which is highly annoying. **But then, all the sudden, there's no noise!** That captures your attention, because there's nothing normal about that. When you hear silence, it makes you sit up and pay attention; it makes you look at the TV to figure out what's going on. That silence shakes you up. It awakens you from that absentminded trance you're in as you watching TV. Because you're used to noise, **the *absence* of noise makes you pay attention.** That's one way to use this principle if you're in the TV commercial business.

With direct mail, this means making your letter look different than everybody else's. You've probably seen good and bad sales letters over the years. You know the difference between them, or at least you can recognize something that looks like all the rest. And most sales letters *do* look the same: they're in the same kind of format, using the same basic structure, so there's nothing attractive about them. **Occasionally you'll see one that's not like everything else you're receiving in the mail, and you pay attention to it.** It could be a postcard, a sales letter with what appears to be handwriting on it, or a lumpy package where you want to see what's inside, because it's not flat like all the other envelopes you receive. These types of things make you pay attention.

Although you can use fonts to your advantage, **I would avoid really oddball fonts because they're hard to read.** That would be a detriment to what you're trying to accomplish. But instead of using a Times New Roman or Courier New font, you might you use a font that looks somewhat different, like Arial or Tahoma. **Another thing you can do is add a lot of subheads that are bigger than normal, or a lot of big blocky paragraphs or very tiny paragraphs.** We've done all these things. We've had one-sentence paragraphs that are never more than one line long, for example. So you might have a whole page of 10-15 one- and two-line paragraphs, because they're easier to read. The paragraphs all jump out a little, too, because they're so small. The main thing is to do things that create involvement.

There are plenty of ways that you can do this. Aside from avoiding excess neatness and other boring things from a design standpoint, **you can also use different kinds of involvement devices:** like requiring them to put a sticker on the order form, or to affix a label to something before they return it, or to check boxes on an application, or fill out various sections, or answer some questions. **You're trying to shake people up a little bit, and make things not as they normally are.** In general, people get stuck in ruts. They get up in the morning at the same time. They get in the same car, drive the same route to work, sit in the same desk, eat lunch at the same time, and have breaks at the same time. Then they go home at the end of the day at the same time, they slip into their favorite easy chair, they eat dinner at the same time, and they go to bed at the same time.

All these things are routine and mundane... and they wear

ruts into people's lives that they get stuck in. Seeing the same ads, and the same kinds of ads, creates the same kind of rut. People become numb to all that neatness and sameness. They don't respond to it, because they've already seen it over and over again. There's nothing there to make them pay attention! **So the more things you can do to shake people up and make them pay attention (without going overboard, of course), then ideally, the more they will respond.**

So get away from the neatness! Dumb your sales letters down! **Get people excited, because bored people don't buy!**

Chapter Twelve

Key to great sales material:

Write lots of copy and edit it down.

Edit, Edit, Edit

The key to writing great sales material is to write lots of copy and then edit it down. This principle applies to every type of sales writing: scripts, magazine copy, direct mail copy, and even websites.

Yesterday, I wrote a four-page letter that's intended as a lift piece—that is, a kind of an insert or flyer that rides along with your main sales letter. But in order to end up with that, I started with eight to ten pages of text—and a lot of very unclear ideas. **During the initial writing process, I just wrote like crazy, getting a whole bunch of different things down. And you see, that's part of the secret.** Not only do you write a lot of copy and then boil it down, but you just go wild during the writing phase! **Never try to write and edit at the same time.** That's a recipe for disaster—kind of like trying to drive a car with one foot on the gas pedal and the other on the brake. You're second-guessing yourself all the time, and the car never really moves that well. It's starting and stopping, starting and stopping—a herky-jerky mess.

So make the initial writing and the editing two separate processes. When you're writing, let it flow. Let it all out. Don't think too much about what you're writing. **Just try to focus on the benefits to the end user—the emotional result of whatever they're going to get from the product or service.** If necessary, teach them why what you're trying to sell them is important; or do whatever's necessary to set up a certain problem so you can offer them your product or service as a solution. **Just get it all on paper (or on screen) without worrying too much about it as you do; then go back and clean it up later.** That's how I do it.

I used to write longhand on legal pads, because that's how my mentor, Russ von Hoelscher, taught me to do it. But that became too painful due to some issues with my hands, so I had to teach myself how to write all over again using a keyboard. Basically, I do the same things with the keyboard that I used to do by hand. In the initial creative phase, I just write. I try to keep an eye on spelling, because I hate to have to go back and fix it, but I don't worry about paragraph breaks and punctuation, and I *never* worry about whether I'm using proper English or not. **I just try to focus on the prospect and the benefits that I want to get across, and why what we're selling is the ultimate thing for them, and why it's worth whatever we say it's worth.**

So when I sat down to come up with this lift piece, I thought about what our new product had to offer to our prospects. The product is called "The Million-Dollar Free Advertising Generator" and it's something we put on people's websites. **First, I had to explain the importance of advertising to them, establishing certain facts about why it's necessary.** Of course, there's all this free advertising out there already, and I had to try to dispel the notion that it's of any use at all. You need high quality advertising, not free junk. Just because something is free doesn't mean anything. If nobody pays any attention to it, it doesn't get any results. **So I explained all that, and then provided a definition of what high quality advertising is.**

I was a little confused as I wrote, but I kept writing like crazy. And then, after about an hour, I sort of hit the wall; which is to say, I ran out of things to write about. So I got up, stretched my legs, and went outside.

It's summertime, so I like to go outside in the mornings. I walked around a little, and while I was walking and thinking about all this, I suddenly came up with another idea—a breakthrough idea that put it all together. That was the simple fact that because it's a free bonus, I don't even *have* to explain how the whole thing works. That was my biggest block when I was first getting started. But I wrote anyway until I ran out of things to write about... and, sure enough, no sooner did I go outside and start walking around than the next idea hit me. **I realized that it's more important to get the benefits across that explain the product in detail.** So later yesterday, I spent three or four hours reformatting those 8-10 pages I wrote and boiling them down to four pages. They're pretty good pages; I'm quite pleased with them.

When you just write a whole lot of copy and don't worry about anything, it gives you a tremendous amount of freedom to go back when you're in that rewriting mode and pull it all into shape. Remember, writing is just one process; rewriting and editing is another. They require different mindsets. **The initial writing phase requires that you just throw it all out there. Don't try to judge, don't try to analyze. The editing/rewriting stage requires critical thought, where**

you're trying to decipher what works best and comparing all the individual points that you've brought to the table. This stage requires a cooler state of mind. You might think of the writing as requiring a hot, excited state of mind, the editing and rewrite a colder, analytical approach.

Even so, the rewriting is also fun—more enjoyable, in its way, than the actual writing. **Both have their moments, good and bad, but when you're rewriting you can be more relaxed.** You can be cool and calm. When you're writing, you have to stay tightly focused on just trying to get it all out. **And you'll find that your best ideas often come in the heat of the moment, after you've been writing for a while.** Once you're all warmed up an hour or two after you start, when you're just writing like crazy and letting it all flow and just trying to get as many words on the page as you can, *that's* when the magic occurs. That's when some of your best writing happens. Then you can take those ideas that you wrote in the second or third hour, towards the very end of your writing session when your ideas started crystallizing and clarifying, and use them at the beginning of your sales material. That's often when you create your best headlines, too.

If you're trying to do it all in one fell swoop, and you're starting cold, then you're really hurting yourself. When you do it this way, you allow yourself so much freedom.

If I write for three hours, I'll end up with this huge block of copy—because again, I don't worry about grammatical perfection or breaking up my paragraphs. But then I can go back through that block of copy and pick out certain sentences and phrases and different ideas that may then work their way up to the front, often becoming some of my best headlines and subheads. **It's all right there. By then, whatever frustration and confusion I had in the very beginning is gone.** Doing it this way just makes it so much easier to know what to do later, when it comes time to flesh it all out and finish it up.

As you put this method into play, please keep in mind that anyone can do this; it doesn't require any special talents. Thinking otherwise—thinking that other people are just naturally endowed with special talents that you'll never have—is disempowering. If you think that way, you're handicapping yourself from the very beginning. Never assume that the good copy you see people raking in the money with just popped out of the copywriter's head fully formed. That's far from the truth. Most of the time what you're reading—especially if you're reading my sales letters!—originated after several long hours of hard work, when the writer had finally gotten into the flow and the writing had finally become red-hot. Then it was rewritten and pounded into shape until it was the best they could produce. **It's not just based on raw talent—it's based on a skill set that has to be developed.**

This concept can translate into a lot of different endeavors. A fiction writer isn't going to sit down and write their best work all in one sitting; it doesn't work that way. A musician doesn't write and perform an entire CD back to back. He doesn't say to himself, "Okay, I need 10 songs on this disc. I'm going to write 10 songs, they're all going to be great right out of the box, and we're going to get right into the studio and record this CD." It doesn't work that way! A musician might write 20-30 songs between CDs, but then they winnow them down to maybe 10 or

12. Authors often write 500 pages to capture an idea, before they narrow it down to the 300 pages that make it into their book. Similarly, a copywriter may write many, many more pages than they need for the final version of a sales letter. **You never know where your best ideas are going to come from, you never know when they're going to come, and you'll never be in a position where the best idea is to write from start to finish.**

I often look over the raw sales copy that I've written, or that Chris has written, and find a lot of redundancy. Now, you may know that I prefer to include some redundancy in my writing, to make sure that I get my ideas across; but I often see copy that's just not needed, or ideas that aren't workable or that need to be tweaked. That's fine; all that can be taken care of in one way or another during the rewrite. **Remember, if you try to edit as you write, you'll lose energy and focus just when your ideas should be flowing like water.** The momentum will fade. As I've said before, the way that you get the best ideas is to come up with lots of ideas; and the way you get the best sales copy is to come up with a lot of copy. There's plenty of time for editing later, so let the ideas flow, let them come naturally, let them cut loose! Accept it all as it comes. Some of it will be great, some merely good, and some will be bad. Capture it all and boil it down later.

That works a lot better than trying to get it just so from the very beginning. **And here's the thing: despite the fact that you may cut out a good half of what you've written, the time that you've spent on it won't be lost, because you can still use a lot of that copy for other things.** You might use some for a lift piece; or perhaps a bit can go on your order form, or be used in a follow-up, or as a Q&A. You can do all kinds of other things with what you've cut out of your original document. Don't think of them as wasted words. **Save the unused content, because you *will* find other ways to do things with it.**

And by the way: **when I'm red hot, I'll try to say something in as many different ways as I can, knowing that I might just hit on the perfect way to say it on the fifth or sixth try—and that I have the freedom to go back and pick and choose.** It's liberating to realize that, especially when you consider how easy the rewriting process is now that we have computers. I've often thought about how difficult those old writers used to have it, compared to the way we have it now. Our ability to make changes so effortlessly on the computer is just incredible—so liberating! We're fortunate to live in this day and age. Imagine having to put a clean sheet of paper into a typewriter and having to re-type a manuscript just to add the revisions and rewrites. That's how the old-time writers had to do it! They might have to rewrite the same damned manuscript dozens of times. I've heard that one poet, several hundred years ago, rewrote the same poem 500 times—500 times! And he was probably writing with quill and ink. Well, it's kind of funny to realize that sometimes, I'll re-work stuff on the computer a couple of dozen times and not even think about it, because it's relatively effortless.

And before I sign off on this Way, let me re-emphasize this point: **stop thinking that other copywriters are more talented than you are.** Get that thought right out of your head! The secret to becoming a good copywriter is the same one I've talked about so often before, in this book and others. **If you've**

got the desire, you can develop the talents. You've got to want to become really, really good. The more you desire it, and the more you're willing to pay the price and follow-up with the discipline, the determination, the focus, and the commitment required, the better you can be. **Talent is nice, but it can't beat a firm determination to succeed.**

Chapter Thirteen

Playing it safe is <u>no</u> <u>guarantee</u> against misfortune.

Don't Just Play It Safe!

Playing it safe is no guarantee against misfortune. It may look good at first glance, but you have to realize that no matter how careful you are, you can't account for everything. **Unforeseen circumstances might crop up, or the economy could tank;** you have very little control over the actions of other people, whether malicious or otherwise.

We have some friends we've known for a long time. They're business people, and consider themselves conservative. They certainly walk that talk, as they say; there's no question about it. But quite often, what they think of as being smart, conservative, and careful, we see as exercises in futility. We believe that as a result of their caution, they've lost a tremendous amount of money that could and should be theirs, ultimately hurting their business more than helping it. **In our opinion, they need to loosen up somewhat, and take a few calculated risks. You should, too.**

Now, I'm not talking about doing something insane, and just blowing your company up. Those situations do happen from time to time. Someone thinks too big, spends too much money, makes foolish decisions—and the company just grows out of control until debt takes over, and pretty soon they're out of business. But for every one of those examples, **I believe that there are tens of thousands of business people who aren't making enough**

money because they're holding back too much.

That's what happens when you're too conservative, at least from a business perspective. Sure, you can be conservative in other areas of your life—but in business you've got to be a little bit wild and crazy! You've got to be a little audacious! **In fact, if you want to make the most money you'd better think about being *very* audacious, because all kinds of marketplace forces are working against your business.** These forces include a bunch of very aggressive, assertive, relentless marketers who'll take business away from you if you're not being that way yourself. You've got to think that way! They're nipping at your heels all the time. You're at war here—at least metaphorically. It's a battle, and the smartest, most aggressive opponent wins.

People who are too conservative think they're being smart, and sure, to some degree they are. **But if you go too far into that end of it**—what I call the defensive end of the game, to use a sporting metaphor—**you can badly hurt your chances of success.**

I like to use metaphors and analogies to think about business and life. It helps makes complicated things simpler; and so, when I think of business, **I think of art, war, sports, politics, and maybe even religion, in the sense that I treat it as a spiritual thing.** I'm committed to it. I'm dedicated to it. And it's easy to mix these metaphors; consider a martial artist who goes to a dojo and spends 3-6 hours a day training and helping the other members of their fight club. In this case, there are both sports and spiritual efforts involved, and that can be true with business as well.

A good sporting analogy would also be football. We're approaching football season as I write, and of course we're Kansas City Chiefs fans. Years ago, we had a coach named Marty Schottenheimer who had the best record of any head coach during the regular season (at least at the time). And we were glad to have him! But he was terrible in the playoffs. Usually, he couldn't advance us very far at all. One year we got pretty far, but I suspect that was because we had an aging Joe Montana on our team. He was a superstar for the San Francisco 49ers, and then he retired and spent a couple of years in Kansas City. But the point I want to make is that Marty is a great man; I'd personally love to meet him and spend time with him. And yet he never could win those big championships for us.

This was true of just about any team he led, with the exception, I think, of a time early in his career, possibly when he had John Elway as his quarterback. **Marty was just too conservative. He focused his entire game on the defense rather than the offense.** The running joke in Kansas City was that if the Chiefs were winning in the first quarter, his whole strategy for the rest of the game was just to hold onto the ball. And, of course, that *was* just a joke—but as with all good jokes, there was some truth to it.

Similarly, people who are very conservative when it comes to business are focused on the defensive end of their game. They're trying to be very careful, very cautious, trying to hold onto the ball the whole time, trying not to let the other team have it at all. To extend the analogy, they're focused on making those 10 yards by the end of the third down. That's stifling and limiting. In football and other team sports, the best teams are the ones that place just as much emphasis on offense as they do on defense. **In fact, some of the most successful teams put a little *more* emphasis on the offensive side—that is, scoring points.**

You see, the job of the offense is to score points; the job of the defense is to keep the other team from scoring points. How can you score in business if all you're focused on is keeping other people from scoring? **If you're constantly trying to play it safe, constantly holding back, you can eventually become totally controlled by your fears.** Well, one of my favorite quotes is, "You can't play the game with sweaty palms." You *can't* be controlled by your fears. **You've got to stay focused on the offensive side of business, which is making sales!** In business, that's really what it's all about: making sales and generating profits. Everything else is support or window-dressing.

I realize that most people are trying to play it safe. **They're watching all their costs so much that they forget they should be focused on the *sales* side of their business.** Ultimately, you have to try to make the most sales for the least cost. It's a razor's edge that we all walk on. The great showman P. T. Barnum once said, "Most people are trying to catch a whale by using a minnow as bait." **People who are too careful, who try to spend less and less money to limit their costs, simply can't attract the highest qualified prospects, because they're not able to tell their full sales story.**

We have a model (built by Chris Lakey) that we're using right now that lets us mail tiny little postcards for very little. We could probably use it for small space ads, too; and yes, it costs us less money than other sales methods. **But then it sends the prospects over to the Internet, where they're asked to watch**

a movie that's 17 minutes long. That's so we can keep the cost of distribution low, while delivering a high-quality, lengthy sales presentation that ensures that we get the best qualified prospective buyers possible.

Admittedly, we're able to do this very cheaply, due to Chris' inspired ideas. But the truth is, once you attract a highly qualified buyer, as long as you're making enough profit margin on the upsell or the transaction, you almost can't spend too much money converting them. **In other words, a big part of the secret of success with business, and Direct Response Marketing specifically, is to spend more money on your follow-up.** That's where all the money is to be made: in converting highly qualified prospects to buyers. Generally, if you spend more money, you'll make more in the process.

Everybody's trying to spend so little to make more money, and yet the real secret is developing the best prospects that you possibly can, telling your full sales story, and then following up in the most relentless, aggressive, systematic way possible. Remember, the idea is to put a little more on your offensive side than your defensive side, assuming you're looking at this as a game. And I think you *should* look at this as a game. It's the greatest game on Earth! **When you're totally focused on sales, all your decisions become easier and more accurate, since now you're focused on what it's going to take to convert this prospect first into a customer, and then into a life-long customer.**

You have to do a complete job of telling your sales story, answering all their objections, eliminating all their fears. All that takes an aggressive sales effort starting with something like our 17-minute movie (which we're getting ready to expand into a one-hour movie) and then a relentless follow-up. We're doing it with live salespeople who can help build those relationships and win their trust. Winning their trust is absolutely necessary if we expect for them to become customers for life.

Don't be like Coach Schottenheimer. Now, he's a big part of Chiefs history, and I admired him personally. I remember the Schottenheimer years as great years—except for the post-seasons. He was a great coach and well-revered and respected as a man who knew how to manage a team and win games. There were a lot of games won under Coach Schottenheimer. But he just could *not* make it happen in the post-season; there were a lot of disappointing years when we made it to the playoffs and lost in the first round. He would point out that there were all kinds of other factors involved, but for whatever Marty did right as a coach, he was known for playing it safe in the post-season especially, and had a very simple strategy of trying to get the lead as quickly as possible and then doing everything he could not to give it up. **It was more of an attitude of playing not to lose rather than playing to win.** That lack of aggressiveness was a big part of the reason he never experienced much success in the play-offs.

This concept that playing it safe is no guarantee against misfortune is one that goes back thousands of years. **Specifically, there's a money principle that's at least 2,000 years old that I think illustrates this point very well: the Parable of the Talents,** which is recounted in both the gospels of Matthew and Luke. The NIV Bible calls it the 'Parable of the Bags of Gold,' but the underlying principle is the same.

Basically, Jesus tells the story about a man who was going away on a trip, so he called his servants together and entrusted his wealth to them while he was gone. One of them he gave five bags of gold, and another he gave two bags of gold, and another one bag, "each according to his ability." The man who had five bags put the money to work at once, and parleyed it into five bags more. The one with two bags of gold went out and earned two more bags.

But the man who received one bag went out, dug a hole in the ground, and buried his master's money. When the master returned, the man who had started with five bags of gold returned the money to his master along with the interest and said, "Master, you gave me five bags. See, I gained five more!" So he gave 10 back to his master. And his master said, "Well done, good and faithful servant. You have been faithful with a few things; I will put you in charge of many things. Come and share in your master's happiness." The man with two bags of gold came forward and said, "Master, you gave me two bags of gold and see, I've gained two more. Here are four bags of gold for you." And his master said essentially the same thing he told the first guy.

By this time, I imagine the third man is sweating a little bit. He's thinking, *Boy, maybe I messed up here!* And so he approaches his master and says, "Master, I know that you're a hardworking man. You harvest where you haven't sown, and you gather where you haven't scattered seed. I was afraid of losing your bag of gold, so I went and hid it in the ground. See, here's what you gave me. I'm giving it back to you now." And the master says, "You wicked, lazy servant! So you knew that I harvest where I haven't sown and I gather where I haven't scattered seed; well, then, you should have put my money on deposit with the bank so at least when I returned, I'd have interest!"

And he says, "Take the bag of gold from him, and give it to the one who has 10 bags, for whoever has will be given more so they will have an abundance. And whoever doesn't have, even what they have will be taken from them. Throw that worthless servant outside, where there will be weeping and gnashing of teeth." Not the prettiest picture, as you can tell. He basically says, "Get out of here, you worthless bum!" Basically, the first two servants were aggressive guys with aggressive investment strategies. They wanted to go out and do something with the money, and take the chance that they might earn even more with it. The other guy wanted to play it safe, because he was worried about losing the one bag he had. He buried it so that at least he would have the one bag, and in the end, he ended up being kicked out and essentially discarded.

Playing it safe is no guarantee against misfortune. Here, the one guy who played it safe ended up being thrown out in the streets—"into the darkness," the Bible says. I don't know what would have happened to him if he'd tried to do something with the money and lost it all... but at least he would have tried to do something. **The master was angry because he just buried the money and didn't do anything productive with it. So playing it safe got him kicked out!**

There are safe ways to promote your business, and there are aggressive, risky ways to do so. **Typically, the results you achieve are in some way related to the level of risk that**

you're willing to take. Now, I do think there are unnecessary risks—the business equivalent of going to the casino and putting all your money on red. You might win big, or you might lose it all. That's just foolish. **A calculated risk, on the other hand, involves studying your market, knowing your prospects, and then aggressively marketing to them based on principles and strategies that you know have worked for other people.** So it *is* a risk, but you've got reason to expect that you can win with it, if you're careful and clever—and, of course, aggressive.

Maybe that means doing a larger mailing than you're comfortable with, or rolling out a hot campaign as fast as possible, risking the money you have in hopes of financial reward for your bold move. That's a calculated risk, and there's an important difference between something like that and sheer recklessness. **Calculated risks are much different from flippant risks where you're just throwing dice or playing the roulette wheel of business, hoping to make a big profit without really knowing what you're doing.** So sure, it's possible to be too cautious in business; though really, there's a wide middle ground between going all-in without looking at your cards and keeping them too close to your vest because you're afraid to take a reasonable chance.

Recently, Chris Lakey and I, along with a few other guys, were out of town together on a business trip. While we were at the conference, we took some time off and rode a zip line. There's a quarter-mile zip line that ends in a platform 100 feet above the ground, and you end it by jumping off that platform. **Well, to take a successful leap off something like that platform, a couple of things need to happen.** Maybe you're over water, and you know you're going to be jumping into a surface that has some "give" to it. You're going to hopefully land feet first at just the right angle, so you don't get hurt. That would be one scenario. Another scenario might be that you're strapped to a harness that catches you and keeps you from smacking into the ground at the end.

That happened to be the case in this example. Without that harness, at the very least you'd hurt yourself terribly falling that far, and you'd probably die. Even so, there's always the faint possibility that the harness might fail. **So you take a calculated risk when you jump off that platform.** Even if there have been no accidents that you know of, the cord could snap! You could be the first person ever to lose his life jumping off the platform... but you know that no one has died so far, so it's a calculated risk, and you have to take it to get down.

There are all kinds of calculated risks in life. For example, most of us drive just about every day; and every time we get behind the wheel, we're taking a calculated risk that nobody is going to hit us and that we're not going to hit anybody, based on our experiences. **Business also has its calculated risks, and there's no avoiding the possibility of risk if you really want to profit.** Conversely, if you decide you're going to play it safe and rule out anything that would be potentially risky or that might lose you money, I feel that you *will* have misfortunes. **And here's the worst part: truly unaggressive, risk-free marketing often ends in failure simply because you fail at the primary mission of business—which is to serve your customers and make the biggest profit you can.**

There will be no profit if you don't take risks. If you

continue down the path you're on, not stepping out at all, you'll keep getting the results that you've been getting; the path leads to the same place every time. That leads to stagnation—or at least to disappointing results, especially if you've set yourself an optimistic goal that just maintaining the status won't allow you to reach. **That's not to say that taking a risk always pays off, because it doesn't.** You might take a risk and just break even, or even lose money. **But the thing about playing it safe is that you don't have any options:** as the old saying goes, you can't win if you don't play. If you choose to take a calculated risk, there's a potential reward for taking that great leap into the unknown. There's no guarantee, of course; **but the fact is, you can't profit much unless you move beyond your comfort zone, into new territory where there's a potential for huge gains.**

So don't pull a Schottenheimer! **Don't be reckless, but don't let your fear hold you back, either. Just be aggressive, taking calculated risks here and there.** Step out on faith, and I think that you'll discover that, in most cases, the reward will be well worth it in the end. Study the success stories of the people who are making it in the biggest way, and you'll see that they're all very aggressive. **It's all about setting huge goals, moving forward onto new ground, and managing risk as you go.**

Chapter Fourteen

The way to sell the *unfamiliar* is to link it with the *familiar*.

Link the Unfamiliar to the Familiar

One of the best ways to sell the unfamiliar is to link it with the familiar: to harness the power of comparison in order to make something new a bit more understandable and appealing to your marketplace. When your constant focus is on doing a complete sales presentation, that means answering all objections, of course; but it also means establishing value. In doing so, you should strive for familiarity, but *never* compare apples to apples. **You should always compare what you have to other things that are far more expensive or valuable. That makes the price you're asking pale by comparison.**

And keep this in mind as you go: **people don't want cheap stuff. They want expensive stuff for dirt-cheap prices!** So it's up to us to give them that as much as we can, while still selling our items at the highest prices that the market will bear. Therefore, the better job you do at presenting the products and services that you're offering in the best possible light, and comparing them to other things that are far more valuable, the more you'll help people understand that the money you're asking for is minimal compared to what you're offering.

And by the way, part of the reason that this principle works is because someone can only know the value of one thing by comparing it to something else. Humans tend to do this automatically; it's part of our natural thought process. We're always comparing things in our mind and weighing their characteristics and value without even realizing it. **All you're doing with your marketing is helping your customers do that.** You're grabbing them by the hand, and showing them that what you have is worth far more than you're asking for it—simple as that.

We have a promotion going right now via one of our advertising and management services. It's for a company that has developed some revolutionary technology, and offers an opportunity to cash in on the cell phone industry. We have a 50-page sales letter that sells this service. **Throughout those 50 pages, there are 13 different comparison charts, comparing what we're offering to what other companies offer.** It's a complete turnkey business opportunity, and in our comparison, we point out all the problems and headaches and hassles that you'd face with a normal business. These charts show people how the other businesses stack up to the one we're offering. The final comparison chart compares what we're offering to a very, very expensive franchise that Sprint, one of the biggest cell phone companies in that world, has on offer. You see, they offer a business opportunity where you can set up a store in a mall—and that will cost you anywhere from $70,000-100,000. We compare that cost with what we're offering. By the time people go through all 50 pages, read about this tremendous opportunity, and then look at some of those comparison charts, they have an idea that what we have is worth all the money we're asking for.

We're doing a full selling job. We're not holding back—and we're not expecting them to do any of the thinking. We're making it easy for them, giving them every example we can think of that compares our opportunity to other businesses that are far more expensive to invest in. **We show them all the headaches and hassles they would normally go through, and how we take all those upon our own shoulders—how we do *everything* for them.** Assuming that they're a qualified prospect to begin with—which we try to ensure with the first step of our two-step marketing system, which gets them to raise their hand in the first place—then by the time they finish that letter, they're likely to make a purchase.

That's just a top-of-the-mind example of a current promotion. **We have another promotion where we compare our business opportunities to a franchise.** Most people know that franchises are expensive—and we tell them exactly how much one costs. They can spend anywhere from $50,000 to upwards of a million dollars on a franchise! And when they do that, they're basically buying four things. They do get a protected territory, which we don't provide. **But the other things that we *do* provide are the same things that a franchise provides:** we have a proven business opportunity, we have expert help that we freely share, and we have a step-by-step system or recipe for exactly what they need to do. And, in many cases, we do some or even all of the marketing for them, and spend our own money on all the follow-up marketing.

Those are the kinds of things you'd find in a high-dollar franchise. We don't expect our prospects to figure any of that out on their own. **We're the ones taking the offensive here, sharing all that with them to help them fully appreciate and understand the true value of what we're offering.** You've got to do the same thing in your business, no matter what you sell.

Sometimes, in order to initially qualify prospects for our more expensive packages, we won't tell them *precisely* what the package costs right at the outset; **but we'll tell them that it's about same as they might pay for a big screen TV, or a home entertainment unit, or a weekend in Las Vegas—or something that would represent a similar value.** We've even compared the price to that of a good used car, so they have that firmly in their minds from the very beginning. We're establishing value by linking our price with something they're already familiar with.

Here's another example, using the same general principal in a slightly different way. Back in the 1990s we sold millions of dollars worth of a special website. Delivering information digitally was brand new at the time, although it's very common today. And then the money they earned was also delivered to them electronically! **So we compared our website with an ATM machine in a bank—an Automatic Teller Machine.** We even went down to our local bank in Goessel, Kansas, and took a picture of its ATM machine—and that picture ended up on page 5 or 6 of the sales letter. We called our websites ATM sites; though our "ATM" stood as an acronym for something other than Automatic Teller Machine, **we still used that visual representation to compare the unfamiliar with the familiar.** Remember, back then the Internet was still fairly new, and very few people had it, unlike today.

Here's another example: earlier, I mentioned that we just came back from a huge seminar. **One of our presenters at that event took something that was kind of old and linked it with something that's fairly new right now: Kindle e-book**

readers. If you've never seen one, they're little machines that Amazon is selling in the millions that let you read e-books very easily. I don't know if you've seen the newer versions of *Star Trek* on TV, but they resemble those handheld readers call "padds" our fictional descendants use. They've only been around for a few years.

The point here is this: **as often as you can, try to link whatever you're selling to the most exciting and newest things that the people in your marketplace understand.** People have to see it to believe it. They have to see it in their mind's eyes, so they can wrap their minds around what you're explaining to them—especially when they can't hold what you're selling. Perhaps in a retail environment, where you're selling a widget that people can actually hold in their hands and examine, this principle would be a little different. But when you sell by mail or on the Internet, or when you sell something that's more intangible like our business opportunities, you're dealing with things that most people can't readily understand just by thinking about them. **Therefore, you have to bridge that gap somehow to connect with them, and to get them to understand what it is you're selling.** If they can't get their mind around that, you're less likely to make the sale. You have to use this strategy to help make the unfamiliar become familiar by comparing it to something they already understand.

Going back to the Kindle, it's a great little device that actually started out being much more expensive than it is right now. They've made it cheaper and better all at the same time, and Amazon now sells some versions for less than a hundred bucks. **It allows you to take something that's thousands of**

years old and thoroughly familiar, the book format, and digitize it, making it into something new. And although Amazon hasn't linked it in their advertising to the little handheld readers on *Star Trek* that I mentioned earlier, I think the fact that a lot of consumers are familiar with those anyway helped make the Kindle easier to accept.

There are a lot of examples that you can use, all through our popular and commercial culture, if you're willing to stretch your creativity a bit. **I like using the franchise example that I talked about earlier.** We use that to help people understand how our opportunities work, because while there are many different things that you can get involved with in the opportunity market—franchises, affiliate programs, multilevel marketing deals, etc.—we feel that the closest cousin to most of our opportunities is the franchise. **Like classic franchisers, we provide turnkey opportunities that give you everything you need. There are no missing pieces.**

In a classic franchise—McDonald's, Starbuck's, what have you—you receive licensing, support, specialty materials and products, and everything else you need to continue in your business. That's very similar to the way we operate—though instead of spending upwards of a million dollars to buy into a business, you can buy into one of ours for as little as a few hundred dollars up to a few thousand dollars, depending on the specific opportunity. **We've also done comparisons with non-franchise opportunities, of course: we might tell people that getting into a specific kind of local business would cost you up to a certain amount.** For instance, you might spend $20,000-30,000 to open a local store of some kind, whereas you can get involved in our opportunity, which we feel is much better, for only $997.

The thing to remember is this: most of the time, when you're selling something by mail or on the Internet, people can't visualize it. They've got no way of seeing it in their mind's eye, so they can't easily judge it. That might cause them to take it less seriously than they should. Of course, you could include a picture of it, and you should, if it's at all possible. You could even direct them to a video online, or something similar. Those are great ways to help bridge that gap. But in most cases, people still aren't going to be able to completely wrap their minds around what's unfamiliar to them, what they've never experienced firsthand. **That's why you need to use things that they *do* know to help them understand what they're about to experience.**

At this conference we recently attended, one of the things that Chris Lakey and a few others did was attend a Mixed Martial Arts competition that was taking place at the same hotel—literally just a few steps down the hall from where our conference was being held. Chris tells me that while he'd heard the name, he'd never experienced MMA before, not even on TV. So he had no reference point, except that he knew there was a ring, and knew it involved people fighting each other in some capacity. They arrived half an hour before the first match, and he was trying to get his mind around exactly what this competition was going to be all about. Is it boxing? Sort of… sometimes. Is it kickboxing? Well, yeah, it can be that. Is it wrestling? Well, sometimes… sort of. Is it Kung Fu? Well, it could be, I guess. It's all these different kinds of martial arts and boxing all wrapped up into one.

The best way for Chris to understand this sport that he didn't have any reference point for was to have a better understanding of the things that make it up. He had seen boxing matches; he knew what that was like. He had seen wrestling—both the fake professional kind, and the competitive kind you do in high school. So he had some ideas of the familiar, some reference points, to allow him to conceive of what might happen in an MMA match. They helped Chris get an idea of what it was like; and sure enough, when the match started, Chris understood what was going on. Understanding sports like boxing and wrestling helped him get his mind around this event, by showing him other examples similar to that brand new experience.

When your audience is unfamiliar with what you're trying to sell, you have to provide reference points to something familiar to them before they can see themselves using and receiving its benefits. **They have to have a connection to something they know and understand. From there, they can make the leap to the unknown; the unfamiliar becomes familiar to them, because you've linked those two things together.** There are still other hurdles and objections to overcome, but if you can bridge the gap, make the new familiar, make it related to something they understand, you'll be closer to the sale.

If necessary, go overboard. When in doubt, do more comparisons than you think you need. It's up to you to make it real. This is especially true, again, if you're selling an intangible like a service of some kind. Some people just use clichés to try to establish value, doing things that really don't make a full impact on the person they're presenting the product or service to. Avoid that. **Focus on building the value, making it real,** helping people see what it is that you want them to see, taking control of the sales process—and, again, making people realize that the money you're asking for in return for your product or service, or combination thereof, is small by comparison to all you're offering. **Go overboard! Paint that picture! Tell stories! Use metaphors! Use examples!** And pay attention to how other great companies are doing this right now. Wake up to the fact that some of the most profitable companies are doing a great job of exactly what I'm describing to you here.

Anybody can cut prices. That's usually ineffective in the end. But it's up to you to establish real value, so that you're getting the maximum amount of money for the items you're selling, so that you're making the maximum profits, and you're making those sales stick. **You're establishing the supreme value of what you're offering in advance, so that when and if buyer's remorse comes along, they won't ask for their money back.** So think that through, pay attention to how other people are doing it, and get really good at doing it yourself!

Chapter Fifteen

It's far better to have a friendship that is centered around the business — than to have a business that's centered around a friendship.

Business is at its best when it is honestly selfish. Strive to keep it that way with all your relationships.

Keep Your Business Honestly Selfish

Business is at its best when it's honestly selfish, so strive to keep it that way. For example: **It's far better to have a friendship that's centered around a business than to have a business that's centered around a friendship.** If you want to have friends in business, then make them as you go along. **Develop joint ventures that are honestly selfish with these friends, where you both know that you're out to make a profit.** Sure, both of you are trying to be generous with each other, but simultaneously, both of you are also looking out for your own business interests. Still, the friendship is very important. Whoever said that business and friendship don't mix... well, that's not exactly true. **Business and friendship *do* mix, as long as you build the friendship around the business. The problems arise when you take pre-existing relationships and then add the pressure of doing business on top of that.** It almost always ends badly.

You probably know plenty of stories like that yourself; the news is filled with them. We have a famous story right here in Wichita, Kansas, involving two billionaire brothers by the name of Koch. Their father started the business, but they've built it up themselves; they weren't just rich kids who sat back doing nothing. They've gone out and done great things with the business. But now there's a family feud, where the brothers aren't speaking to each other. They've been warring back and forth in court for years and they hate each other's guts and they communicate only through their lawyers. Stories like that are commonplace.

Business is stressful. Business is demanding. **When you add the stresses and complexities of business to a pre-existing relationship, you've got a recipe for disaster.** I've got some stories from my own life that prove that—where I went into business with friends, and lost them along the way. With me, it began with my very first sales job. I was hired by a good friend of mine, Ron Shepard... or at least, he was my good friend until he became my boss. He thought I would make a good salesperson, and ultimately, he did teach me how to sell.

Ron was a sales manager for a company out in Colorado Springs, Colorado, so I moved out there. I'm very, very grateful for the fact that he was a friend of mine, that he looked out for me, and he hired me as a salesperson. I'm an avid reader, so while I was on my first sales job **I was reading millions of books on sales, and I was really trying to get good at it, trying to learn it as a profession.** Ron taught me a lot. Because he was a friend, he had great influence over me. He believed in me and he encouraged me... and he let me get away with whatever I wanted to get away with. **He gave me special favoritism, in fact. I was one of five or six of his sales reps, but he treated me special, and all the rest of the sale reps knew it, and it caused lots of problems.**

A handful of years later, Ron and I went into business together—and our friendship quickly dissolved. The business ended that friendship completely and totally. We haven't spoken now in close to 20 years, and I'm convinced that it was because of our business venture. Who knows? Maybe we would have gone our separate ways anyway; but the business was that final thing that killed our friendship.

I started my very first business in December 1985 with my good friend Gary Purvis. **Gary was my best friend then, and in one sense at least, he was a good influence.** If it hadn't been for Gary, I would have never started that business. I would have been too frightened to do it! Luckily, Gary had all the qualities I lacked at the time. He had no fear, total confidence, and total courage. I mean, he could sell anything to anybody! He was afraid of no one. **As for me, I had all kinds of fears and insecurities and doubts... and Gary just paved the way for us. He made it happen, and it was great.** We had some good times, and we both learned a lot. **But again, the friendship was destroyed.** It got to the point where I felt I was outworking him... and this has happened to me time and again. I'm not saying I'm right, but I always I feel like I'm outworking my business partners.

Now, these days I'd say that I'm doing it by choice. These days, I would say that I'm doing it because that's who I am. It's not their fault I'm outworking them. And these days, I have greater respect for people and the overall value they bring to the table—and I know that sometimes, the amount of work they do isn't nearly as important as the quality of their ideas. **So I'm a little smarter now than I was 26 years ago... but I didn't wise up until after that friendship went downhill.** I still value that friendship greatly, even today. Without Gary, I never would have gotten started on that path.

Those pre-existing relationships can be wonderful for a

while, and partnerships are extremely valuable if you're new at something and you've never been self-employed. I can't think of a better way to get started than to have a business partner, because you're sharing all of the initial joys and frustrations that go with it. **So friendship *is* very important**—but the reality is, those friendships I mentioned are no longer.

Working with family can be disastrous as well. My sister Ann and my brother-in-law worked for our company for a while, and that never worked well. I was so glad to get rid of them. **My wife Eileen has had a few family members who worked for our business, and it was best that we went our separate ways.** Having them working for us caused problems with my marriage. The only reason my marriage has worked with the business in the first place is because from the very beginning, when I first started dating my wife, we were doing business deals together. By our third date she was working with me, side-by-side. Back then, I had a carpet cleaning business. One day, I couldn't come over to her house in the evening because I had a restaurant to do, and she said, "Well, let me help you with it!"

So she went out on those carpet cleaning jobs with me. She and her little kids, who were 7 and 11 at the time, would go out with me, and the four of us would flyer parking lots and we'd put flyers on doors. **So Eileen and I started working together almost from the very beginning, and her kids were involved in the business too. I think that had something to do with the fact that our business has, by and large, been a blessing for our marriage.** It's created some problems, sure, but it's created a lot more good than bad.

Later, my Dad came to work for me. **I only hired him because I felt sorry for him, since he was retired and wasn't doing anything with his life, and he was just wasting away. By the end of the first day, I knew I had made a *terrible* mistake.** It took me four or five months to get rid of him, and it just wasn't good. He got on the job and just started farting around and doing nothing. He was just shooting the breeze all day long! All he wanted to do was BS with the rest of the employees, which created lots of problems.

Don't hesitate to find good joint venture partners within your marketplace, but keep your friends your friends and your family your family. The pressures of a business can do a lot of damage, even break a family apart. There's a funny Jack Nicholson movie called *About Schmidt* with a few great scenes about business and friendship, by the way. Family members got other family members involved in some crazy Multi-Level Marketing scheme, and it became a real sore subject for the whole family. Well, when I first got involved in Network Marketing, even way before I started my first real business, I lost some friends by trying to sign them up to all kinds of crazy deals—by exploiting my personal relationships, like they tell you to. It's a disaster! It's no good!

But let's talk about the good stuff: joint venture partners. This is where you come together with another entrepreneur to do business. They're looking out for themselves and you're looking out for yourself, but both of you are trying to add value where value didn't exist before. That's the essence of joint venturing, at least when it really works. **You're bringing something to the table they don't have,**

they're bringing something to the table you don't have, and if it works, there's a synergistic reaction between the two that verges on the magical. Some of the people I joint venture with I consider to be my friends, because joint venturing with them is so fulfilling and profitable. Now, looking at friendship in that context might cheapen it in some people's eyes, but not in mine; because, to me, the business is my life, and my life is the business. And it's about a lot more than just making money, even though I do love that!

Speaking of which, when I was younger and dumber (not that I still don't have a lot to learn), I used to read stories about all these really rich fat cats—the Billionaire Boys Club, so to speak—who wanted to do business only with other rich fat cats. If you weren't a fat cat, there's no way you'd ever end up in that circle; it was closed off to the rest of the world. I used to be so jealous and resentful about that. **But you know what? I get it now, because I've got my own inner circle.** If you want to be part of it, and you want to joint venture with me, it might take you a little while to get into that circle. You'd have to really work at it. I think that's how it is with a lot of wealthy people. They find good people they enjoy spending time with, and they do mix business and pleasure and friendship; and naturally you want to do business with people you like.

We had a seminar in Branson, Missouri, just a couple of weeks ago. My joint venture partners and I were all walking to supper, and there were some really cool customers of ours walking ahead of us. We'd just spoken with them in the hotel lobby before we started walking to the restaurant, and you know what? I really wouldn't have minded having dinner with those customers. I love my customers! But I was with my joint venture partners, my friends in business, and so to me there was no choice about it. **I love my clients, but I love my joint venture partners even more.**

I have to say that **I'm starting to see what I think of as an ugly trend in marketing; and it's most obvious on the Internet, where people have joint venture partners but everybody's got these email relationships going on.** And that's all they are: they just email back and forth. They've never met each other and they've never talked to each other on the phone, so these are shallow relationships by my way of thinking. Maybe I'm old school, but I just finished spending a lot of time with some of my joint venture partners, Chris Lakey included. Five of us rented an RV and we drove down to Branson together. That's a six-hour drive! So we're 12 hours in an RV, the five of us, and these are people I really feel a connection with. **They're people I consider to be my friends and my peers and my equals, and I got to spend valuable quality time with them.** I think this growing trend of people who want to do everything online, and want to keep their relationships confined to emailing and texting back and forth—I don't think it's a good trend.

I try to keep in personal contact with my friends in the business—my good friend Ken Pedersen, for example. Every month or so, Ken and I will get on the phone for three hours at a time. Of course, it helps that we're the same age and we like listening to the same music and watching the same movies. We have commonalities other than the business. **But whoever said business and friendship don't mix... they're wrong! We just**

keep the business our number one priority, and our friendship is fine. So business and friendships **can** go together, and even go together well. But to reiterate the main point, it's far better to have a friendship that's centered around the business than to have a business that's centered around a friendship. Business is at its best when it's honestly selfish. Strive to keep it that way.

Let's take a closer look at that "honestly selfish" concept. We live in a society that, for the most part, believes that selfishness is a character flaw, that the idea that you might look out for your own interests first is somehow wrong or bad. There are people who believe that all business is predatory—that a business that's looking out for its own best interests and trying to make a profit is somehow preying on people. Along with that philosophy comes a belief that anything you do for selfish reasons is suspect. And certainly, there are questions about whether we should be selfish as individuals; so selfishness is not necessarily a positive character trait. **But in business, you really do have to be selfish, in the sense that you have to look out for your own interests—and you need to establish a hierarchy or pecking order of importance for your business based on those selfish motives.**

Now, you might say, "A business that's only looking out for its own best interests doesn't really care about its customers," but that's not true. In fact, that's the farthest thing from the truth, because a businessperson who's striving to make profits knows that his customers are fuel for the fire. **A selfish entrepreneur is very in tune to what his customers want or need, because his profits come from those people. So yes, it**

***is* essentially selfish to take care of your customers, which may sound a little backwards.** But the selfish motivation for profit means that you do what you can to serve your customers well and keep them as happy as possible, because you know that your selfish motive for profit only lasts as long as you're able to keep your customers coming back for more. This is true whatever the industry, whatever you sell.

I don't want to go too much down a political rabbit hole here, but I'll give you an example that I think illustrates my point when it comes to business. There are people who say that the government needs to own all the remaining wild areas throughout the U.S. that haven't already been turned into cities. There are some states that are vastly owned by the Federal Government, actually, and there's very little private ownership except in some small cities in those areas. One of the biggest reasons you have a lot of environmental advocates saying that the government needs to own this land is because, they say, that's only way to protect it. Their argument is that if you left it in the hands of commercial enterprise, there would be no parks left; the entire landscape would be all businesses, high-rise apartments, and, in general, concrete jungles.

And in some cases, that may be true. But it isn't always; and I would argue that it isn't most of the time. Consider, for example, the paper industry. Do you think the paper industry has a selfish profit motive for making sure there are plenty of trees? Of course they do. It's natural that a paper company would want tree farms to thrive. And so they want some kind of an ecosystem to exist where they can plant new trees, have them grow, harvest them, and make their paper products. Ditto for the limber industry, which needs new building materials. **So there's this self-perpetuating desire to protect the environment, so those trees can continue to grow to a size big enough to be chopped down.** There's a profit motive for those businesses in that industry to see to it that the forests exist.

Consider the commercial fishing industry. Do people pollute the oceans? They absolutely do, no question. But I can guarantee you that commercial fishermen don't want that pollution in the ocean. They have a profit motive for making sure those fish are as big and plump and healthy as possible. People who harvest crabs and lobsters, do they want fishing nets lining the ocean floor? Absolutely not. **There's no profit motive in them in destroying the environment they need to make their living.** So there *is* a selfish commercial motive for them to keep the environment healthy.

In contrast—and again, I don't mean to make this political in nature—if the government owns something, it's not necessarily as well taken care of. Let's say some bureaucrats have turned some land out in Arizona into a wildlife area. Do you think the average Joe walking through that park cares about whether he drops some trash on the ground? There are probably some people who do, who are very sensitive about those things. But the average person doesn't care. They've got no vested interest in the place. The way to keep the environment healthy and clean is to have private ownership, because you tend to take care of the things you own. The same thing is true of government-owned housing. If the government is paying for your housing, you have less of a vested interest in making sure your roof gets repaired or a toilet gets fixed.

Private ownership and, in this case, a business profit motive—honest selfishness—drives people to take care of the things that are providing their livelihood or keeping a roof over their heads. **In many ways, business is at its best when it's honestly selfish, whether you're talking about relationships or private ownership of property.**

To backtrack to the initial point, it's far better to have a friendship centered around business than to have a business centered around a friendship. I watched a TV show the other day that I think was a good illustration of this principle. The premise of this particular show is that there's some restaurant that's not doing well, and it's probably going to close if something major doesn't change. The host of the show comes in and shows people how to fix their restaurant and get back on the track to profitability, restoring their hopes and their dreams of being in business for themselves.

In the episode I was watching, there were four partners running a sort of bar and grill together. They had a full bar area with high-def, big-screen TVs and the overall bar atmosphere, but it was a restaurant where you could get food too. This was their dream, and these four guys were all buddies who had gotten into this business together. Well, over the past several years it had driven them apart. The business was suffering, and they all blamed each other. Now, they all had different things they brought to the table. One was the bookkeeper, for example, and another was the marketer. I'm sure when they got started they thought, "Hey, we're all great buds with great talents. Let's go into business. Let's make some money together!"

But they were on the path of blowing up their friendship,

barring this intervention—and I don't know what happened after the cameras left. I'm sure that had things not changed, they all would have gotten angry and left, and the business would have closed down. That friendship that was so important to them would have been destroyed, because they got into business together, and the business took over the relationship and became a stress point which ultimately led to the failure of both the business and the friendship. I'd guess, based on the look of them, that they were probably in their 40s. So maybe they'd been best friends since high school or college. Who knows? But fortunately, at least as far as I could see, they got the ship righted. **The show's host came in, and showed them some things they could do to freshen the place up and make their restaurant profitable again.** They gave their restaurant and bar a complete makeover, and the new people who came in after that loved it. It seemed like they were on the right track. Hopefully they got it straightened out, and they're doing well today.

I've seen other cases where friends went into business together, and it didn't work out. Often, it just drives a wedge between them, damaging the relationship they already had. So, you have to be very careful when getting into business with friends. I'm not telling you to abandon your existing friends when you get into business, but usually it's better to keep business and existing friends (or family) apart. Once you're in business, you need friends who can help you; so look for people in the business you can connect with, who can be your support system and help you be the best you can be.

I've mentioned this road trip we just took to Branson in an RV with a few business friends. We spend the whole six hours each way talking about business and life. **The business friendship is different from a casual friendship, but it's just as important as any friendship that you had before you got into business. These friends joint venture with us.** We invite them to speak at our events. We work with their customers, and they work with ours. We sometimes just go around and talk shop about what's working and what isn't, and they offer support and an ear, and they're always interested in what's going on because we've established a friendship through the business.

There are a lot of people we deal with who, if it weren't for the business we're in, we'd have no relationship with. Oh, maybe we would have met them at some point, and they would have become friends through some other channel, but as it relates to our businesses—well, if we weren't in the same or similar businesses, there would be very little likelihood that we would ever know them. **Some of our best friends in business live clear out on the coasts, some over in Georgia and Florida, some in Texas and Arizona, and all over the U.S.; places we might not be inclined to ever visit, just on our own.**

In fact, one of our good friends is from a city in Georgia. Chris Lakey drove his family to Disney World several years ago, and drove right through that man's hometown. Until then, we had no clue where his town was. I'd never looked it up on a map. I just knew about it because we've done business with him, and we've been JV partners over the years. Sure enough, as Chris was driving down the highway in his minivan and came upon this town, he was like, "Oh, hey, here's this town that Michael lives in!" Prior to that, Chris had no idea where it was. **So outside of the fact that we had this business**

connection, we probably never would have run into Michael, much less have become friends with him. And yet, through the business, he's become an invaluable resource, and hopefully that friendship will last a lifetime.

Those are the two options. Option A is have friends and get into business with them. Option B is to get into business and then find friends in the business. Option A rarely ends well. There are all kinds of business problems that can rip apart an existing relationship. The better way is to start your business, keeping your existing friends at a distance (at least businesswise), and then find likeminded people in your business or similar industries to connect with. And they don't necessarily have to be in the same industry: In our town there's a group of young entrepreneurs whom I believe are called Young Professionals of America or something similar. There are probably branches of that society, or similar ones, all over the country. They get together every month, have lunch, and talk about their businesses.

You can make friends there, too, with people who are in other industries but are nonetheless like-minded entrepreneurs. **They often have business interests and goals in common with yours, and can become your biggest cheerleaders and supporters, because they understand what it's like to be in business, and what you're going through.** Your old friends might not. They may be along for the ride because they want to help you out, but often they're not really supportive, because they've got no idea what it's like to be in business for themselves. So if you do mix friendship and business, remember that it's much better to have a friendship centered around the business than the other way around.

And remember that being honestly selfish in business is not a bad thing. Your selfish ambition is what gave rise your business in the first place. **Once you've started, your selfish desire to make a profit drives you to serve your customers in the very best way you can, by finding as many ways as possible to give them what they want, so you can get everything *you* want.** So looking out for your customers is a selfish thing in and of itself, if you care to look at it that way.

www.ingramcontent.com/pod-product-compliance
Lightning Source LLC
Chambersburg PA
CBHW020204200326
41521CB00005BA/238